PRAISE FOR NO APOLOGY NEEDED

Your book is fabulous. What a great tool—so much great advice. This book provides tangible advice for success in leadership. From assessing your own leadership behaviors, identifying signals where change may be necessary and doing this all through honest reflection. Nicky reminds us that all great leaders lead through authenticity. We all bring uniqueness, biases and past experiences to the table. This book offers valuable advice in assessing your team: aligning your team's goals with organizational strategy, conducting a team skills assessment, and assessing your team's org structure for optimal performance.

—Tammi Desens, Financial Leader

Seriously, a beautifully written book with a clear message about being your authentic self, why that's important, what it means if you're not, and how to get there. Each chapter brought something new that really challenged me, made me think, and most importantly, gave me information and tools that I can use to become more authentic myself. Nicky shares personal details and tells her story beautifully. She sends a clear message that your leadership is guided through not only what happens at work, but what happens in all aspects of life. Don't ignore that part of your life. Embrace it! I can't wait to hear what Nicky's doing next!!!

—Melinda Rice, Program Leader

Nicky does a fantastic job with this book. It's easy to digest and her authentic self is relevant. It supports the reader in a positive way. The book is GREAT!

–Julie McAdams, Education Leader

Nicky Espinosa is a dynamic and authentic change agent. Her book illustrates her no-nonsense approach to living one's truth. Nicky engages the reader immediately. Her words inspire; her messages motivate us to level up our careers and amp up our goal-attaining efforts. By implementing concepts in this book, I've learned the importance of cultivating a new mindset. Her words shed light on the dichotomies women experience: she makes vulnerabilities look strong, trepidations look fearless.

–Christine Gruber, Healthcare Advocate

NO APOLOGY NEEDED

THE CAREER-TRANSFORMING POWER OF AUTHENTICITY FOR WOMEN LEADERS

NICKY ESPINOSA

Special shout out to everyone who contributed to the making of this book.

Editor: Jen Boysen

Cover and Interior Design: Andrea Schmidt

Early Reviewers: Dan'elle Watkins and Tammi Eickhoff

ISBN: 978-1-7378336-0-4 (paperback), 978-1-7378336-1-1 (ebook)

If you enjoyed this book, please review it on the website where it was purchased. *Thank you*!

CONTENTS

INTRODUCTION

This book is for all the dreamers. The young women who grew up imagining a world full of possibilities. Those who worked hard, got an incredible education and found themselves in a career that held them to a different standard than male counterparts. This is for professional women who've experienced gender bias, double standards, and the subsequent drive to prove yourself beyond reason. Some of you can share recent experiences that sound like they came straight out of 1975. It's ridiculous, and it needs to stop. Hold onto your high heels, Ladies.... things are about to get real.

I've coached many executives over the years who come to me looking for trusted counsel, but they ask for tactical advice. They say things like, "I can't get my team to (fill in the blank)," "My board doesn't understand the complexities of (fill in the blank)." They want advice to fix an immediate problem. These are surface level fixes. To truly develop yourself as a top-tier professional and dare I say as a person, you need to go deeper.

For most of my career, I mainly coached male leaders. There were just a lot more men in leadership positions than women. But as workplaces progressed and more women were finding their way into positions of leadership, I focused all my energy on supporting women.

When I shifted my focus, I found that the women I work with are interested in much more than the tactical. They want to build strong problem-solving skills as their foundation for personal and professional growth. For them, it wasn't enough to develop into a great leader. What they really wanted, was to learn what being a great leader specifically meant for them. These women wanted to be themselves and stop conforming to the style of leadership that their male predecessors were using. They wanted more authenticity.

For a long time women have been taught to act like and be like the successful male leaders before us. But what if the way those leaders acted was not what made them great?

My passion is to help women leaders lean into their own authenticity, find their leadership style, and confidently take their seats at the table. And yes, that means we need to learn to navigate through some bias and bullshit behavior. My purpose became very clear to me when I made the decision to help as many women as possible. Early in my coaching business, I successfully worked with both men and women. But the men that I worked with almost exclusively viewed the experience as transactional. They wanted to check a box, learn a skill, and tell their promotion panel that they were committed to constant learning. They were more interested in either solving an immediate leadership dilemma or looking good for their boss. That just didn't float my boat. I can certainly coach you to become a great leader, but if you aren't interested in growing personally, I'm not interested in working with you.

Today I only work with women. Women who are leaders or aspiring leaders. Women who want to make a difference. Women who are smart, capable, and compassionate. Women who need a little help to navigate the ridiculous glass ceiling that still looms. I made a choice to do everything I can to put more women in positions of leadership, influence, and power. Not because I'm an angry feminist (though I get pretty worked up about some of the stories my clients share), but because we need more women everywhere that decisions are being made. Preach RBG! I believe a balance with representations of all genders, race, ethnicity, and world experiences at the decision-making tables will make this world a better place. And women haven't gotten that opportunity in the same ways as men. I want to be a part of changing that...one woman at a time.

This book is not about bashing men. Some of my best mentors have been men. Some of our greatest advocates are men. I had one male client my first year that really got it. He did the personal work. He accepted my critique and took accountability. He called our work together the most profound coaching of his career. And most importantly, he made changes that pivoted the course of his career and brought him great joy and fulfillment in his professional and personal life. And then he became one of my biggest supporters, helping me develop my marketing strategies and grow my network.

Men will play a part to help us shatter the glass ceiling. We need more men in power who recognize the sexism and discrimination that still happens in most workplaces today. Both men and women need to call out when things are not ok and correct them. Transformational changes need to be championed from positions of power. Until more women are in those positions, we need the men already in those positions to advocate.

But that doesn't mean we don't keep pushing from wherever we are. In fact, that's what this book is all about. How to influence from your seat, how to navigate the political waters of a male dominated profession, and how to do so with confidence.

Oh, and if you're a mother...no worries, we are going to address the sheer mountain of responsibilities you have on top of your paid work. You can build the career you want and be a mother; don't let anyone tell you otherwise. You just need to set your rules, and I'll show you how.

Here's the first thing you need to know: embrace all the parts of your life, especially the really messy parts. In my experience, our personal lives have not always had a place in our professional lives. We have been taught to leave our personal stuff at home when we go to the office. This was particularly misaligned for a lot of women.

The last decade has fostered an appreciation for authenticity. It has become more acceptable to be yourself at work. The fake face of leadership can be put away. That means you are going to bring the things that are on your mind at home to work with you. If you try to shove them down or compartmentalize them, you may find the personal things that have your attention will come out sideways at work.

I truly believe, and live my life with, the promise that you cannot be two different people at work and at home. Anybody can fake it for a while, but when things get tough you can no longer keep them separate. As a woman leader I didn't feel like I could be my true self at work for a long time. And I didn't talk about work much at home either. I tried to live two different lives. And because I tried so hard to keep work and home separated, I wasn't my best in either space. Pretending I was two different people took all my energy. It took some really tough lessons for me to understand it, and I'll share some of those in the next chapter.

As you embark on this personal journey for yourself, take inventory of all the parts of your life. You are a product of your experiences, and your impact on this world is greater when you bring all your experiences with you. We are going to talk about everything you need to be a great leader. There is a lot of good stuff here that you can put into action tomorrow. But it won't mean as much if you aren't able to lead with your whole self.

I'm going to tell you about the messiest parts of my life and how they made me a better person and a better leader. I hope that you can take what you learn from these stories and your own experiences to always bring authenticity to everything you do. This is not about being like all the other leaders before you. You are unique. You are special. Yes – you are different and THANK GOD! Because we need more of you. Your stories make you real. When you can be real and you know how to lead, you can move mountains, my dear friend.

1

MY STORY

L et me start by telling my story. I've always been a driven person. I excelled in school, breezed through college, got the job I wanted, married an awesome guy, and started a beautiful family. I believed that I could have anything I wanted if I just worked harder. I was confident and assertive, and led with a positive attitude. I came into a room like a tornado (in a good way). I knew I had a positive impact on people around me, and I was ready to take on the world. I had built the beginnings of a seasoned career in business, specializing in organizational effectiveness and strategy execution. I know – sounds fancy, right?

On the surface, it looked like I was living a great life, and in many ways it really was. My marriage was happy, we had two great kids, and were blessed with incredible friends. My career was progressing quickly. I had landed a great job at the best employer within 100 miles. I owned a home, a decent car, and we could go out to eat with some regularity. Things were good.

But things aren't always as they seem. I felt guilty that I wasn't fulfilled with all that I had. I felt selfish and embarrassed to say to anyone, "is this all there is?" I loved my life, but something was missing. Like a puzzle, that missing piece in your life does not minimize the other pieces; it's just missing. When you look at a puzzle with that one missing piece, you often don't notice it right away. If you squint or just ignore the gap, you can almost see the full picture or even pretend it's complete. My life was that puzzle. I didn't look for the missing piece. I told myself that I needed to be content with the rest of the pieces.

But here's the thing, when you ignore something that you know in your heart is missing, you cut your spirit. Over time those tiny cuts get bigger or scar over, and either way they leave a mark on you. You've heard the tale of the woman on her death bed with all the ghosts of her unfulfilled dreams around her. All those dreams that she pushed down. I told myself, I'll do that later, when the kids are grown, when I have more money, or when I have more time. What if that time never comes? You'll be at the end of life and will have never found your missing piece. For me, the thought of that regret was strong, but not strong enough to divert my path. I was too focused on the kids and my career path that I thought I was supposed to be on. I told myself that I needed to focus on the beautiful things in my life.

It could just be the normal course of life, but as I buckled down to be the perfect mom and wife and employee, I became focused on the wrong things. For me, the "perfect mom" did all the right things, so I followed the advice in the parenting books and did what my parents did through hard work and discipline. I turned my children into projects. I tried to manage them into adulthood. Lunches were packed, they were dropped off (never rode the bus), assignments were done always before dinner, and a fully balanced meal most nights. I was also driven at work, so I put in the extra effort, made the bold moves, and got noticed. My husband worked nights during this time of my life. Seriously, this gave me a free pass. I was allowed to ignore my marriage under the pretense that "we are doing our best on opposite shifts, can't wait until he works days!". Spoiler alert... Free pass is not free forever.

And then I got tired. I started feeling the cracks in my armor like many mothers of pre-teens. Those cracks are painful, but they allow you to explore below the surface. I wasn't equipped to explore those parts of myself during that time of my life, so I responded to those painful cracks by letting them scab over, putting on a bandage, and sealing them up. Then I told myself to suck it up and keep going.

I'm a fan of motivational speeches, and I love to listen to podcasts. I enjoy building up my audiences at my speaking engagements and hope to do even more of that in my lifetime (avoid that deathbed regret!). For me, positivity is motivational. I hate hearing a speaker who is yelling some 'get your shit together' rant at their audience in the guise of motivation.

I realize that negative shaming works for some people, but not me. You can yell at me all you want, and I'll just shut it down. However, during that particular time in my life, I was struggling and didn't have any positive motivating messages coming at me. Instead, I was trying to take advice that was screamed at me like it came from a football coach. "Just keep going!" "Work harder!" "No one is going to do this for you; get up and get it done!"

So, what did I do? I pushed on...and the universe knocked me down, *hard*. The next five years were the most difficult of my life.

THE GIRL:

I remember it well. I was tidying up in my daughter's bedroom. She had been growing up. She was "dating" a boy, and at age 14 didn't know much about dating. I really didn't worry. This was a "meet at the movies and hang out after school" kind of thing. I had noticed her getting a bit withdrawn but wrote it off as typical teenager stuff. That day in her bedroom I found a piece of paper, folded haphazardly on her dresser. I thought it was garbage, but something in my heart drove me to look closer. It was the beginning of a very dark description of her world. I would not quite classify it as a suicide note, but it scared the crap out of me. It was one of "those moments." When you take a breath and lean on all those parenting books you read. Maybe you call a friend. Over the course of the next month, I confronted her and tried to understand. To be honest, what I was really doing was trying to understand enough to fix it. Looking back, I'm ashamed to say I was more focused on a tactical fix-it activity rather than truly being there for her. It hurts to write those words. My daughter is one of my favorite people in the whole world. She inspires me every day. But back then, she was my kid, my project, my job to raise. I thought if I could just read another book or talk to another therapist I could figure out how to fix this problem. I told myself I was smart and driven. I can do anything! HA!

I hired a therapist for my daughter. Ok, it was actually several therapists. When I didn't think she was progressing enough with one, I'd hire someone else. That pattern repeated again and again. I watched her like a hawk. I checked her phone, monitored her friends, and did my best to 'fix' it. Even with all of those things put into place to help her, she wasn't getting better. I learned she was cutting herself, a self-mutilation outlet for her internal pain. My beautiful daughter was folding into herself. The light that used to shine so bright within her was dimming. And although I was losing the battle, I spent the next year in denial. The perfect family that I had envisioned was not my reality.

Looking back, that's such a crock. I wish I'd understood that the family I wanted was not about outward appearances. It was about the people I love having inward contentment and strong family bonds. That only comes from understanding each other. REALLY understanding each other. And you won't ever completely get there. It's a journey, and I'm now enjoying the ride.

But back then my personal journey was guided by my daughter and later my son. When I stopped trying to fix problems and started appreciating life's moments, I found a happiness for them that is deeper than anything I could have imagined.

But back to the story...a few months after I found 'the note,' I got a call at work from an emergency room nurse. She said, "your daughter's here; she's fine. I just wanted you to know." My whole day blew up, and I thought, "What the hell?" My daughter was 15. She was at school. Cheer practice was at 7 a.m. I saw her off to her day. Now it was 3 p.m. and apparently, I had no idea what was going on in my child's life. Massive parent-fail! The worst part? The nurse couldn't tell me anything. At age 15, Gabby was old enough to choose not to let me or my husband know why she was there. We found out that she did not want to see us. When she was ready, she would contact us, but until then, she would be admitted into a unit in the Generose building. I worked for this hospital. I knew what was in the Generose building, adolescent psychology. I went there to see my daughter but was not allowed admission. I stood in that hallway, looking through windows into the unit and hoping to catch a glance of her in there. I just wanted to make eye contact with her so I knew she was ok. It was a low point for me.

Luckily, I have amazing and brilliant friends. My good friend Lauren listened quietly and said the thing that I held onto, "She is in a safe place. Tonight, you don't have to worry about her hurting herself." OMG, I hadn't realized how bad this was, and I had missed all the signs. I had been so busy trying to fix things and to build the picture of the life I wanted, that I had completely missed them. I called my doctor and freaked out with what I now know was a panic attack. I asked for good drugs to help me through. He said, "Have a glass of wine and relax." On the surface, that was a completely reasonable prescription. But I was from a family of alcoholics. Probably not the best advice for me. I'll tell you more about that later.

This was the first of three significant hospital stays and intensive outpatient therapy for Gabby over the next 18 months. We learned of the trauma she had experienced, and they were big things that she didn't feel like she could talk about. It was heartbreaking. You don't want anything to hurt your children. Then something inevitably does. If I could rewrite her history and take away the pain I would, but that's not how this works. I can't fix this. What I can do is walk beside her, feel her pain, feel her joys, gently guide, and let her walk her own journey. Scary shit huh? I grabbed another bottle of wine to get me through.

THE BOY:

While all this was happening with my daughter, I also had my son at home. Chris is two years younger. He's a sweet, super smart, quiet boy. He was "easy" in many ways. But when one crisis happens it can cover up another one. I would learn many years later, after Gabby was off to college, that my son's struggles were deep. He, too, had experienced trauma that I hadn't known about and he hadn't shared.

I still have a lot of guilt about not knowing, not noticing, that my children had endured these extreme situations in their teen years. I had missed the signs of Gabby's trauma. Chris hid his pain so well, and yet I still felt, as a mother, that I should have just intuitively known there was something amiss.

As I started to understand trauma, depression, and anxiety, I saw how much was out of my control. I didn't know how to deal with it.

During Chris's teen years, I was dealing with a toxic working environment that would ultimately result in my boss being terminated for harassment. I threw myself into the bottle. I liked to think that unwinding with wine at the end of every day was classy. But let's be honest, I was simply self-medicating. I was numbing my own pain, worries, and the other emotions I didn't want to feel. And for a while it worked. I felt like I could endure my days, if just for the wine. But that's no way to live. And it took me down a dark hole that meant I wasn't there for Chris when he needed me to notice he was struggling. Another epic parent-fail.

There are days that change your life forever. What I share with you next is a story that shook me to the core and began changing me, both personally and professionally. One morning, I got up earlier than usual and rushed into work. My boss, the king of harassments, had been in tyrant-mode and I needed to get to the office before him. My son was downstairs, sleeping in his bedroom. He was 18, no need to check on him. But as I left the house that morning, I felt this tug to look in on him. I pushed it down. I left. Another moment in my life that I replay.

Chris was in his bed, overdosed on sleeping medications, in an attempt to end his life. Three hours later, thank God, he woke up and became alert enough to call for help. He called me at work. He was scared. He wasn't making any sense. I was confused, but I understood that the situation was dire. I stayed on the phone with him on the drive home. He seemed to have difficulty processing what I was saying. The ambulance got to our house before me. The EMTs said Chris was going to be ok, but I was devastated. How could this be happening?

I remember sitting in the emergency room, the feel of the faux leather seat and wooden arms of the chair, solidly supporting me as I listened to the psychiatrist explain next steps, hospitalization, medications. I felt emotionally numb. And too calm. Later, I let myself break down and then I dealt with my own emotions and doubts through therapy. Therapy taught me so much about processing trauma, loss, and stress.

After Chris's hospitalization and intensive therapy, he met the woman who became his wife. Chris got married and secured a good job. On an individual level, he is still putting in the work to understand himself, heal from past trauma, and build his life on his terms. That is hard work, and I'm so proud of him. As a mom, the day of Chris's attempted suicide was the most difficult day of my life. It could have been so much worse. The doubts crept in, and I beat myself up. How did I miss the signs, again? After Gabby's struggles, I should have known what to look for so something proactive could have been done for him.

Although my brain overanalyzed the days leading up to the attempt, the morning of the attempt, and everything afterwards, it also led to some healthy self-reflection. Struggles aren't always seen on the surface, and no matter how close you are to someone or how much you love them, it doesn't guarantee that you'll see their signs of distress. This was a difficult lesson for me to accept. I know now that I was not at my best at that point in my life due to my own issues, and I've made peace with it.

You may be wondering, "Nicky, why are you sharing these personal stories about your children with us? What does any of this have to do with women and leadership?" It has everything to do with leadership. To lead with our most authentic selves, we need to understand how personal experience impacts each and every one of us so we can better relate to those we lead. The truth is everyone has their own troubles. Some are deeper than others, but you can't compare. You just need to accept that we are all dealing with tough stuff.

THE ADDICTION:

Let's talk about my "classy" wine. As I shared earlier, there was a period of time in my life when I found great comfort in my nightly bottle of wine. Yes, I said bottle. Does that sound bad to you? Hold my...um...sparkling water, and I'll share my story.

Both of my parents are recovering alcoholics. I watched my mother go through intensive inpatient treatment for her addiction in my early teens. Addiction is a bitch, and it took our family a long time to heal.

I had succumbed to the same addiction. Even though I knew my risk. Even though I knew the power of addiction. I thought I could handle it. I could not.

After realizing I had a problem, it took me another year to put away the wine. Therapy helped. Friends helped. My husband was my rock. But the climb out of addiction is another struggle that I share with so many professional, intelligent people.

How is it that someone who is incredibly intelligent and well-educated could succumb to something as simple as addiction? It's pretty simple actually... addiction really is a disease. Addiction is widely defined as a chronic brain disorder and disease due to effects on the brain and body. Like many illnesses, the level of suffering one experiences as a result of the disease falls across a wide spectrum.

I suffered, still do suffer in recovery, from this disease of alcohol addiction much in the same way that my friend Connie suffers from Lyme disease and another friend has cancer. I know some people will have a hard time with those comparisons, but unless you have lived through addiction yourself, you don't get a vote

When I realized that my wine habit had become an addiction, I was devastated. I ignored it for a very long time and convinced myself that I was justified to drink at the end of every day. I was a hard-working professional, an over-stressed mom, and I deserved it. That's what I told myself, and I fell for it.

As the drinking increased, the blackouts became more frequent. The toll on my body was showing, and my husband gently pushed me to acknowledge my problem. At a rather timely couples therapy session, my husband dropped the topic into the mix, and all hell broke loose. I was so incredibly angry. We were there to talk about the kids, not *my* problems! We've been together for 26 years, and I can't remember ever being as angry with him as I was that day. He was trying to help me, and instead, it made me rage. I didn't see it at the time, but looking back, his courage that day was a tremendous act of love. And my response was the worst I had ever been to him. That is what addiction does to us; it grabs hold and wants to be fed, but it also wants to be denied. It often parades around in the real world looking like normal behavior. Most people only see the first 2 glasses, but your family knows the truth.

Even after the infamous rage-inducing therapy session, it took me another too-many-months to find the courage to take my very last drink. I tried to quit six times. Relatively few attempts, considering that I know others who've tried fifty times. This is why we are always *recovering* addicts. We are taking one day at a time. We are praying that we don't succumb to the temptation for that sweet glass of wine. And we don't judge anyone for falling off the wagon because we know that we are all just hanging near the edge. Some are closer than others.

Because I've been open about my family's challenges, I know now that almost everyone has some form of trauma in their lives.

Depression, anxiety, and addiction run rampant in my family tree. What was once sheltered and not talked about in my family circles, was there all along. Hidden doesn't mean absent.

My children have taught me so much. I know they have a LOT more to teach me. They are the most authentic, accepting, loving young adults. They have embraced who they are. They accept people with open hearts and genuinely want to understand other people. They are open to possibilities. Don't get me wrong, they are still young adults, but they are going to be ok.

2

THE WHOLE YOU

I tell you these deeply personal stories because I know we all have a story. It's part of us, integral to who we are. You will bring your story to your work. You can't avoid it. You can hide it for a while. You might even be pretty good at hiding it. But it's there. Whether it's a divorce, addiction, grief, finances, mental health......everyone has something. It will color your work. Imagine a clean, bright white canvas is your work. Now imagine everything in your life is paint flying all over the place. No matter how excellent your canvas protection ninja skills are, the paint will get everywhere. You can't stop it. You can't separate it. Over time those colors will create a beautiful picture, and the canvas is never the same.

Now here's the kicker... if your life is so perfect that your canvas is bright, white, and pristine.... you will suck at leading others. Or rather others will not want to follow you. We don't accept marriage advice from the couple who just met last week. Nor do we trust leaders who are not "real". We need to embrace those things that have created this amazing person that is you. Accept your story, however traumatic, and be honest first and foremost with yourself. The best leaders take everything they are, everything they feel, and add in the smarts. That's a powerful combination. People will follow those that they relate to and trust.

I'd like to make an important distinction before we discuss relating to others. When I talk about people you *relate to*, it does not mean people who are *like you*. This is a diverse world, and we are better together. The root of human existence is a commonality that spans across oceans, races, religions, sexual orientation, etc. At the heart is your heart. Every human being has a deep need for acceptance, validation, and love. Your traumas are not unique. I don't mean they are insignificant. No one escapes this life without some kind of trauma, and there are others who share your brand of it.

I'm urging you to be your whole self as a leader. Be authentic. Be real. People will relate to you when you're honest about who you are, all of you. You've heard it said before, and it bears repeating. There is a wisdom that comes with age. Yes, and so do scars, bruises, aches, and pains. And we learn from these too.

Leading with your whole self doesn't mean going against your nature. If you're not comfortable sharing your personal life at work, you don't have to tell your team everything you did this weekend. You don't have to share that you're going through a divorce. *But you do need to accept that these are a part of who you are.* Your acceptance of yourself, with all your beauty and flaws, will affect how you relate to others. It affects all your relationships, personal and professional. You don't need to tell your colleagues everything you're going through, but you will not achieve your greatest life without some vulnerability.

As you explore what changes you might need to make in your life, ask yourself what you want. What do you really want? This is not an easy question to answer. If you answer it too quickly, you probably aren't giving this enough thought. Those of us who've lived through some shit get really clear on what we want. You have to add some color to that page. You need some scars to find that clarity. So don't worry if you don't have it down quite yet. Just keep working on it. Look for the things that you feel in your belly. Those are signals guiding you to the best YOU that you are capable of becoming.

After my son's suicide attempt, I made a decision to be completely honest with those closest to me at work. This meant my immediate team and a handful of peers that I worked with regularly, about 30 people, were going to see the real me. I was scared I'd be sacrificing my credibility as a "solid leader" with my personal stuff, but I was at a point of not giving a flip. My son had attempted to take his life. Suddenly, my peers' opinions of me didn't mean so much. The boss that was a tyrant, I was done putting up with his shit. You quickly separate the people you care about from the others around you. I told myself I wanted them to understand what was going on so they could help me with my team. I needed their help, and it felt right to tell them. I crafted a well worded email and hit *Send*. Then I took a nap.

When I woke up, I had received full support from everyone. There were emails and phone messages, and I knew I had anything I needed from them for the coming weeks. That felt great, but I also learned an important personal lesson. I was suddenly not trying to be two different people. I was just me, all of me. I was sad, scared, and brutally honest about it. I took a couple of weeks to work through some things. The day I returned to work I walked into a team meeting in progress. This was my team meeting that my Program Manager was leading in my absence. I came in a little late. If I'm being honest with myself, I had been avoiding it. Even with all of the support, I was still afraid of what they really thought, both about me and what I'd shared.

As I walked in the room the entire meeting stopped. My colleague approached with arms open and gave me the best hug ever. There were tears, there were cheers of support and encouragement, and ultimately this was a moment that I will never forget. My team was incredible. Over the next year I had many experiences like this, though admittedly with fewer tears. I talked with co-workers who shared their own battles with addiction and suicide, struggles with kids, depression, finances, divorce, you name it. I learned that my vulnerability, which just felt right at the time, was what we needed all along. I was a great leader before this, but after this I was a *real person* and found that I was enjoying leadership even more. I found that I was full of joy and had even greater compassion for others. Leading with authenticity, bringing my whole heart, gave a renewed purpose to my leadership. It made me better. I wasn't like all the other leaders. I did it my way. And it was good. I created a lot of positive changes in that team. I made a difference in truly meaningful ways for our organization. I felt like I had found my secret weapon.

3

GAINING YOUR LEADERSHIP PROPS

Ok, so you understand why I say you need to bring your authentic self to all you do. Let's talk about gaining the necessary leadership props. You need to be able to get the job done. That means understanding your business. Whatever your industry, you'll need to know the ins and outs. Take the initiative to learn as much as you can. Shadow your teams, learn the processes, read everything you can get your hands on, interview other leaders, in short do everything you can to learn. One of the most important factors in considering multiple internal candidates for promotion is subject matter expertise. You need to know your stuff. Studies have shown that men tend to have greater opportunities for mentorship when it comes to the details of the business. Don't accept this as your fate... go get the training you need to expand your specific knowledge gaps.. Ask for mentorship, ask for projects that will give you experience with the details.

When I took a role working with the Department of Laboratory Medicine and Pathology at Mayo Clinic, I didn't know anything about the work of the department. I only knew what I had experienced as a patient; I would get my blood drawn, and my doctor would read the results. What happened in between at the laboratory was a big mystery. So, when I needed to lead a team of project managers to support this department, I wanted to learn more. You could argue that I didn't need to know the details of the lab to be able to do my job, and you would be right. You don't need to know every little detail, but you do need to understand the big picture and how the departmental areas work together.

While I didn't need to know how to run a lab test, it was tremendously helpful to see how it all works together. To understand the high-level process flows, the different roles of the talented employees, and the overall challenges of the area was invaluable. I accomplished this by interviewing leaders, shadowing lab staff, and taking tours of some of the biggest areas. Gaining this understanding made me better at my job. It's a competitive advantage you should not leave on the table.

I see a lot of women feel like they don't know enough to pursue the next level. They opt to go back to school to earn another degree. While education is valuable, and if you love school, go for it... don't expect a degree or certification to completely fill the knowledge gap you perceive is holding you back. In my opinion there are two major reasons to pursue education for career advancement.

Pursue the appropriate education and certifications that will 1) ensure you meet qualifications for the roles you want and 2) teach you foundational skills that help you do the work.

You might also pursue additional education because you love learning, enjoy the classroom, and want to do it for yourself. More power to you.

Before you go back to school ask yourself which of these are your goals. If you can't confidently articulate what you're getting from the experience, it might not be worth the investment.

You might be surprised to hear this but learning the tactical tools of leadership isn't the hard part. Education offers are widely available today. Almost any professional can choose to get a degree if they are willing to invest time and money. It's not where the secret sauce comes into play.

Become well-versed about the pertinent details of your organization, both the ones necessary for your job and the big picture of how it all works together. There are no excuses for not learning your organization. Pursue the best ways to learn about it, and understand that it's not always going to be solved by returning to school.

Understand your organization. Learn the secret sauce. These are your table stakes.

Know your stuff. The rest of this book focuses on the hardest parts of being a leader.

4

SIGNALS

Once you know your stuff, leadership happens with the people around you. Leaders are charged with fore-seeing the opportunities, anticipating the risks, and dealing with the problems. The hard part of leadership is knowing what to do, when to do it, how to communicate, and getting an entire team or organization of people to follow your lead. This is NOT easy. Sometimes the easiest way to start to see what you need to do differently is to examine what it looks like when things go really wrong.

I've spent 25 years coaching people through a lot of mistakes and made a few myself along the way. Let's dive into a few "what not to do" stories, and I'll share how some simple pivots can propel you towards the leader you want to be.

Before you continue...make sure you are ready to be honest with yourself. I want to share with you, over the next few chapters, all the mistakes I've made and the ones I've coached other leaders through. You will get the most out of these chapters if you can be self-reflective and brutally honest with yourself.

Now that you're ready, let's talk about signals. Most of us don't expect to be terrible at the hard work we put forth. If we take the job, accept the promotion, or tackle the challenge, we do so because we think we can do the work. We have probably told ourselves that we will succeed. There is a big difference between confidence rooted in competence versus arrogance blinded by ego. The arrogant ones don't think they are arrogant. What if you are the arrogant one? Would you know?

It seems like every time I attend a large conference and listen to a leadership speaker, the audience is always the same. It's a sea of leaders and aspiring leaders looking for validation that they are worthy. These sessions are often motivating, usually have a nugget or two of wisdom, and often leave the audience excited to go back to work. There is nothing wrong with these types of speakers or their content. I enjoy a great motivational speaker. Most are natural story tellers who have developed into skilled orators, and I have deep respect for them. But we leave the conference, and the impact of this speaker is often short-lived. Leaders go back to their organizations and lives, and they likely do nothing differently as a direct result of the conference speaker's message.

I want you to view these experiences through a different lens. Look across the audience. Who is engaged? Who is taking notes? Who is scrolling on their phone? I'm not interested in judging someone's choice to engage or disregard the speaker, but let's think about what people are taking from the experience. I find it fascinating how many times we sit in those audiences and have someone in our mind that represents all the crappy traits that the speaker is highlighting as poor leadership. Admit it – you do it, too. The speaker talks about the leader who lacks vision; you think of someone very specific. Maybe you have several in mind. Many people in the audience are doing the same. You can see them as they nod and smile or laugh at the ridiculous things. They make eye contact with their colleague across the table. They are thinking of the same person. Sometimes after the session they commiserate. They might say, "That speaker was right on the mark, I wish John was there. He really needed to hear that. "

What if John was there? Do you really think he would have learned anything? John doesn't think of himself that way. He thinks he's great. Everyone else is the problem.

So, what if you were John? Would you know? This is the hard part. You need to be able to critically assess yourself as a leader to grow. Even if you find it difficult to be self-reflective, other than to validate yourself, there will be signals that you have blind spots. Look for the signals. If you see them, pay attention. If you don't see them, ask for some objective observation. Chances are you have blind spots. Spoiler alert: we all do!

There are signals all around you. Signals will tell you a lot about yourself, if you are willing to listen and truly examine how they relate to you. Pay special attention to any signals that indicate you're leading with less than your whole self. Think of signals as gifts. They are gifts to you only if you pick them up, unwrap them, and do something with them. For the next several pages we'll review some of the most critical signals that, when recognized early, can allow you to make changes that will build you into a better leader.

SIGNAL #1 – YOU'RE EXHAUSTED TRYING TO HAVE IT ALL

All too often, you go through the motions. You strive for the promotion because you believe that it's the natural progression of your career or it's what's expected of you. You buy the next house and the next, forever upgrading because it tells the world that you are successful.

Your personal life is the place where you've pretended to have more choice, but let's be honest. How you choose to spend time away from work is deeply influenced by values that were rooted in you at a very early age. You grow up, go to college, get married, have kids, blah, blah, blah. Live the dream. Or maybe your path was to graduate high school, get a job, get an apartment, pay taxes, and visit mom on her birthday. The path looks a little different depending on who instilled those values in you. Make no mistake; we all learned what the path was "supposed" to be before we entered grade school. Depending on whether the instilled values fit with *your* values, you may feel like you are an actor, playing a part in your own life. To really live your life, you need to feel passion, energy, and joy in the work and life you choose. This doesn't mean you are always happy or spring out of bed every morning like a character in a Disney movie. Life is hard. We all feel that. We all get tired. But are you ALWAYS tired? Pay attention to that. It is exhausting to live a life where you are always "on," always playing that part that you think you are supposed to play.

Some of this way of responding to our lives is so deeply rooted that you may immediately dismiss it and not realize it should be examined. It's scary to really look at yourself. But know this...you can't be a better leader if you ignore the colorful parts of the canvas. Remember the paint is getting everywhere.

You are kidding yourself if you think you can be one person at work and a completely different person at home. The bigger question for you is, "why would you want to?" If you are putting on an act for any part of your life, it's no wonder you're always exhausted.

Take some time to really let that question sink in.

When you're ready to look, really look, at the signals, then you might be ready to be a better leader, friend, partner...person.

Signal #2 – YOU'RE LISTENING TO YOURSELF TALK

One of the most important signals to notice is how much time you spend talking. Do you talk 50% of the time? Do you spend an hour meeting talking 'at' the team for 55 minutes and then ask, "let's do a quick roundtable – anyone have anything?" This is a trap that's easy to fall into, even for good leaders. When there's a big project or problem to solve, especially when deadlines are approaching, it's not uncommon for leaders to revert to *directing* rather than *leading*. And there are circumstances when directing is necessary, such as military responses, life or death decisions, and crisis response situations. How often do you run into these situations? In my 25-year career, I can count on one hand the experiences that called for this kind of response. The reality is most of us don't need to do all the talking. In fact, it's detrimental to the team, builds walls, and cuts the leader off from their most valuable asset: the collective knowledge and skills all around them.

It's easy to identify whether you are spending too much time talking. Just pay close attention to your actions and your audience's reaction.

There are several tactical steps you can take to control your verbal contributions. Structure your meetings by building in plenty of time to allow others to participate. Unless you are presenting something very specific, try to avoid talking more than half of the meeting time. In some cases, you might even need to talk less.

The biggest problem is that incessant talking behavior negatively affects the team. You'll need to watch for signals from your team. When you spend the whole meeting talking and set very little time aside for the roundtable, you send a very clear message. A message that's probably the opposite of what you're trying to send. You inadvertently send the message that you don't care what the team has to contribute. You're effectively saying that your contributions are more important, and ultimately, you don't really have time for members of your own team. In short – you send a message that you don't value your team. Why would anyone want to work under your leadership?

If this is you, unpack why you're doing all the talking. What are you trying to avoid? Are you trying to control the conversation? Have you considered that you might not trust yourself to navigate an unstructured conversation, including tough discussions, that might come from the participants? If there is fear, what's it based upon? Why do you fear? What does that say about you and your own limiting beliefs about yourself? By welcoming your teams engagement you align your behavior to demonstrate confidence. When you are a confident leader, in yourself, your teams, and your organizations vision/strategy, your teams will follow.

The other possible reason for your excessive contributions may be that you really like to talk. Maybe you enjoy the presentation. Maybe you enjoy the attention. There is a time and place for you to let your presentation skills soar, but it's generally not in your team meetings. Check yourself, and work on it.

Signal #3 - WHAT TYPES OF QUESTIONS DO YOU ASK?

Another signal to examine is based on the types of questions you are asking your team. Are you asking them very tactical, "just the facts, folks" questions? You need to get updates and understand what's going on in their work, but do you really need all the details? In my experience, the only time I really need to understand the details of a team member's work is when there are performance issues. With that said, most of the time people detest this kind of micro-managing.

Sometimes a manager will tell me that they need to know details so they can decide how to help their teams. The intention here is good but is never well-executed. In fact, your real issue may be that you are not sure how to lead the team, or said another way, you are not comfortable leading at a higher level without the details. This says more about you as a leader than your teams. The outcome is that you will micromanage the details to make yourself feel more in control of your role. Your teams will feel that micro-management, and it will translate into the message that you don't trust them to do their work.

This leads to resentment and frustration from even the most chill employees. No one wants to be micromanaged. You don't want to be micromanaged, so don't do it with others.

A frustrated employee will spend a lot of energy getting you all the details and trying to make you feel comfortable, rather than actually getting the work done. Productivity will slow. Turnover will increase. Recruiting will be challenging when word gets around that you're always in their business. And you rarely will find anyone to go the extra mile for you.

Think about it this way, if you tell me exactly how to do my job and then watch and make sure I do it exactly as you've instructed, then I don't need to think. I don't need to try. I'll do just enough to get you off my back and not a stitch more.

When I talk to leaders about their management style, no one ever says they micromanage. This term has such a negative connotation that most leaders vehemently deny this kind of behavior. Some will even try to explain to me how their type of (micro)management is necessary. They say things like, "I can't trust them to do it right," "I'm the one who's ass is on the line," or "they just don't care enough." Make no mistake – you are micromanaging. It does not work. You will not succeed this way. The end result is a team of people who will not come through for you.

I know it's hard to acknowledge this might be you, but if you see any of these signals, you'll only benefit from taking a hard look. If you find you need to make some changes in this area, I suggest starting with a self-examination of your motivations. Don't just accept your first thought, dig deep. Ask why, then why to that response, then why again. Figure out what is necessary for you to feel confident that your team is producing results. Your past experience will drive your confidence. If you were let down in the past when someone didn't share information with you, this may cause you to require detailed information in order to feel confident.

Micromanaging is usually rooted in the manager's own insecurities and inability to trust others. This is some deeply personal stuff. It's usually very difficult for someone to dig into this on their own. You're too close. Having an objective partner, like a coach, can really help you uncover the things that you can't see objectively. If you recognize a few signals that you might be micromanaging, don't ignore them. Work on them. Beyond the employee morale challenges here, you'll find that you will struggle to stay focused on the most important strategic priorities the higher you advance in your organizations. As your workload increases, the urgency of daily problems can dominate your schedule. This makes it difficult to keep focused on the strategic priorities. Don't ignore this signal!

Signal #4 – HOW YOU SPEND 1-ON-1 TIME

Think about this for a minute: If your 1-on-1 time with a team member was just 15 minutes how would you spend it? Again – think about who is doing the talking. This is their 1-on-1. They should be doing the talking. You are there to coach them and learn what you need to do to help remove barriers for them. It's easy for these conversations to become tactical updates on their work. When you don't set expectations for the meeting, your employees can assume that you want their work updates. Some employees will want to give you a list of everything they are working on. At first this might seem appropriate, but it's surface level stuff. You will get tactical updates. You won't learn what's really on their minds, what they are dealing with, and how you might be able to help. You'll get data that's not actionable.

Another mistake a leader may make is using one on one time to give their own updates. It's never a good practice to try to communicate team messages to one person at a time unless the topic is specific to that person or impacts them personally. Think of it this way... you wouldn't want to go to each team member's desk to personally tell them that you are changing the weekly report format. Your message will be inconsistent, and it will take a long time. However, let's say you need to communicate that a key member of your team has resigned. You may want to communicate 1-on-1 to the people most closely impacted by the resignation before you communicate more broadly.

Be clear about what you intend to come out of the 1-on-1 meetings. I suggest the following objectives:

1. Understand your team members, their motivations, and their burdens.
2. Look for ways to help them.
3. See patterns across the team that you want to resolve or improve. This information will help you set strategic goals for your team.

I promise you no leader actually thinks that they may be talking too much in 1-on-1 meetings. They may acknowledge that they talk a lot but not accept that it's a problem. So, I want you to really self-reflect here just like I've asked you to do with every other tip in this book. You might find yourself talking more than you want and more than you thought! Sometimes you might feel like you're trying to encourage communication by filling in the silence. It's an easy trap to fall into. If you feel like one of your team members is just not engaged, rather than fill the gap, ask more questions. Practice making them comfortable. Try different environments like an informal standup in the cafeteria instead of a sit down meeting in the boardroom. Or different ways to communicate between meetings (email updates, daily newsletter, etc.) that might help them feel more prepared. And give it time. Trust takes time to build deeply.

In my corporate world, I loved 1-on-1 time with my team members. In my business, my personal coaching sessions are some of the most meaningful work I get to do. But it's not easy for every leader. If 1-on-1 time is not comfortable for you the team will cue into it. Your best approach is to examine what makes you uncomfortable and work on yourself. Consider what makes you uncomfortable and work on rewriting that story for yourself. If 1-on-1 time is strange for you because you once had a bully boss who berated you every time, you may need to release your emotions from that experience to be present for your employees now. If you're more comfortable they will be, too. This takes me back to one of my key messages about authenticity; just be yourself. Understand that you have history, baggage, and a story, as does every member of your team. Use your 1-on-1 time to learn their stories and understand how you can help them at work.

This relates back to Signal #3: What types of questions do you ask? 1-on-1 meetings can be the most crucial time for asking the right questions. How you choose to spend this time with each team member can mean the difference between engaged, satisfied employees and disgruntled, low performers. If you don't care about them, they won't care about you. The worst thing you can do as a leader is create an environment where your employees don't care.

Use your 1-on-1 time to engage with your team members. Genuinely care to understand them. You can't motivate anyone whom you don't take the time to understand. I challenge you to ask more thoughtful questions and engage your team members in discussion about their responses. Remember this is their time, not yours. They should get something from this meeting. Best case, they leave feeling valued, committed, engaged, and inspired. I know this seems like a tall order, but nobody ever said leading was easy.

For those of you who find 1-on-1 meetings really uncomfortable, find conversation starter questions that you can ask. Focus on identifying three questions to start. As you begin to understand each team member you can tailor your questions to each person. The questions should keep the focus on the employee; remember a successful 1-on-1 is measured by the employee, not you.

Questions I have successfully used for 1-on-1 meetings:

- How are you doing?
- What's on your mind today?
- What's your focus this week? (Word of caution: This should not be a dissertation on *everything* they are tackling this week. You may need to guide them to help lock in on their main focus.)
- I know last time we met you were having trouble with "Project A", how's that going this week?
- How do you feel about the progress of "Project A"?

- Do you have any thoughts about how we might fix "Problem C"? I would really like your input.
- What's keeping you up at night?
- Is there anything that's frustrating you?
- Is there anything I can do to help you?
- Are we meeting frequently enough? Should we continue this cadence, or try something different?

Ok – so let's say you are not loving your 1-on-1 meetings and/or you think you might be talking too much. GREAT – you've acknowledged a weakness, now you can address it!

Explore why you might be falling short. What are you thinking before, during, and after the meeting? How do you feel about doing the 1-on-1? Some managers really don't like these engagements. They find them uncomfortable. I hear things like, "it's not worth my time." Remember, it's not about you. Yes, your time is valuable. Yes, in the big scheme of things you might have some other pressing matter that you'll need to deal with this afternoon. But this is their time and if you don't make it theirs, eventually no one wants to meet with you either.

On the surface, this looks like a win to the manager who hates 1-on-1s. Bonus! My employees don't like these meetings either. I'm off the hook!

It's not that simple. Poor 1-on-1 meetings and generally insufficient interpersonal interactions with your team is a ticket to turnover. People don't leave jobs; they leave bosses. Your job is to grow their skills, help them find their potential, and make them want to work with you and the team. Messing up the 1-on-1 interactions is like trying to call the neighbors without a telephone. You might be able to exchange some communication screaming from your yard, but it's not likely going to be fulfilling. But if you invite the neighbors over, have a BBQ, laugh, and exchange stories, you've built a connection. People who love their neighborhood have a much harder time moving to a new place. The community and connection they feel is valuable. Your teams are like that, too. Are you the neighborhood everyone is trying to escape from or the one where they love to live?

Most leaders who avoid 1-on-1 meetings do so for two reasons; either they don't find them valuable because they are thinking about themselves, or they find the interactions uncomfortable. Maybe your reasons are different, but the vast majority of leaders I've counseled fall into these two camps. To grow your own leadership skills in this area you don't need to push through these meetings. The just-make-it-happen approach has its time and place, but this is probably not the time. Because human beings are innately aware, they will KNOW when you are not being genuine. So, don't just push through, but work on yourself, prepare useful questions, and figure out what you don't like about one on one time. Work on you...so you can be a better leader for them.

Another note regarding 1-on-1 meetings:

Avoid rescheduling 1-on-1s as much as you can. In our busy schedules, it's very easy to move a 1-on-1 to allow for a more important meeting or one with many participants. This is generally accepted, but it is best practice when you need to move a 1-on-1, especially on the same or next day, that you reschedule close to the original time. Don't say, "Sorry I can't meet today, but we'll connect a week from Thursday." Not cool!

Signal #5: ARE YOU ASKED FOR YOUR INPUT?

I have a great friend whom I trust deeply. When I need advice, she's my person. I know she'll be honest with me, and she'll give me great advice.

She has two very important qualities. I trust her to have my interests at heart. She knows me well, cares about me, and wants me to be successful, too. I know that her input is always given with the intention to help me, even the tough stuff that's hard to hear.

My friend is also a great leader. She knows her stuff. I respect her work and know that she is highly competent. If she gives me advice, I know she's also sharing her knowledge with me. And because I think highly of her, I want to learn from her.

This brings me to the fifth signal, how and when your team asks you for input.

When someone genuinely wants your input, you need to have these two factors in place 1) Trust and 2) Respect. If you haven't earned your team's trust and respect, they won't ask you for your input or they will appease you by asking for your input with little intention of taking it.

Don't assume you have trust and respect.

This seems so simple and yet it's often missed. Leaders assume that they are trusted and respected just because they have the title. This is a huge mistake. As workplaces progress and employees demand more from their leadership, many leaders aren't adjusting. If you rely on your title to give you respect you might get the opposite, no respect, no trust, and you might find yourself the butt of jokes.

I had a few managers over the years that didn't understand this, but the most prominent one was Brenda. She had several roles over the years and did have some impressive accomplishments. She had built an entire department from scratch to provide support services to the organization. Sounds impressive, right? But the reality was she was a figurehead. A lot of times other people deserved the credit for those accomplishments, but she took credit and got visibility across the company.

The further up the ladder you get in your organization, you risk losing perspective. This can occur for a lot of reasons, but in this case, Brenda had lost all perspective of how she was perceived by her teams. She was so concerned about getting accolades from her superiors that she focused on pleasing them and only them. It didn't really matter to her how her team was feeling or thinking, as long as they did their work and made her look good. She put on the right performances and tried to say the right things to her teams, but she often fell short.

I'm making this sound pretty clear, but don't get me wrong... Brenda didn't see that she was doing this. She said the right things when she was presenting to them or talking about her team to others. But she couldn't have a meaningful conversation with her team. Any interaction was strained. She fumbled over what to say and often offended her teams. When polished and prepared, she looked like a great leader, but when being herself, especially when unscripted, her true nature showed. She fumbled for the right words. She over-compensated and gushed her compliments, so they sounded insincere. In short, she was so worried about impressing her bosses that she couldn't be herself. Because her bosses were her priority, her actions were NOT focused on the best interests of her team. And her team saw everything.

She became the subject of many jokes. Her team meetings were painful. Because she didn't do well with interactions, she used every team meeting as a platform for presentation. She spent the entire time presenting to her teams. She did all the talking and left very little time for interaction. In this way, she could control her performance. And that's all it was... a performance.

I remember the day I learned about the way the team felt about her. At first, I felt vindicated. She frustrated me every day. It felt good to know that I wasn't alone; others were seeing this behavior, too. But then I felt sad for her. She didn't know any of this was happening. I thought about telling her, not all the ugly details, but at least giving her some feedback. Unfortunately, I didn't trust her either. So, I couldn't be real with her. And she had already made it clear to me on other topics that she was the boss and my input was "appreciated" (that's what she said) but was not valued (proven by her actions – nothing). So, I didn't say a word. Her career will be summed up with being the butt of jokes and convincing herself that she's right and all her teams were wrong.

Your team's interaction with you can tell you a lot about how you are perceived. In Brenda's case, she was occasionally asked for input, but not regularly, and the request was often to appease her need to be involved. Sometimes her team asked for her input to see what she was thinking so they could avoid rework when she didn't like what they had done. This request for input is not from a place of respecting your opinion but covering their own butts.

So, ask yourself....do your team members or peers ask you for your input? I mean, do they really ask you? It doesn't count if you offer your advice or insert yourself into a project or discussion. You are looking for someone reaching out to you apart from any other reason to interact with you, just to ask you for your input. That's valuable. Many leaders will brush over this and say, "oh yeah, I'm asked for my input all the time." But when you ask the team, they say "hell no!".

This disconnect is pretty common in leaders. I meet people all the time who have one idea of how they are perceived, but we learn something very different when I do 360 assessments for them. They are often surprised and confused. They wonder, "how did I get so disconnected?"

It happens because of the stories you tell yourself. You may be inserting yourself into discussions and offering your opinions because you want to show value. Not because your opinion is sought out. It's an important distinction. If you are always offering and they are never asking...the hard truth is what you are offering may not be valuable to the conversation or to the teams. Or you may be offering something of value, but they don't trust or respect you so they can't see the value.

You can have the water that they need, but if they think it's poison, they aren't going to drink it.

Once you can differentiate genuine interest in your input, another thing to consider is how often you're asked for input. You can't count that one time two years ago when someone asked for your input. When you are a respected leader you can expect someone will reach out to ask for your input regularly. If this is not happening weekly or monthly, you might need to take a pause and ask yourself why. Go back to trust and respect. These are things you need to work on with your team. Building trust and earning respect happens through relationships and competent performance. Put your energies here to start to improve in these areas.

Now let's look at the type of input. Also consider if you are being asked for input or rather direction. This is very different. You may be asked for your direction around every corner. This is actually a different kind of signal related to micromanaging that we talked about earlier. If you feel like your teams can't make a move without you, this is likely more correlated to a culture where they fear making a mistake.

Teams who are in need of constant direction are not the same as a team genuinely asking for your input.

We also want to watch for how your input is considered. Is your input sought and then easily tossed aside? What you want to watch for is a team culture that asks for your input to appease your ego or to shut you up. It's simple manipulation, but it happens. You'll need to deal with your ego or lack of respect from the team. These are tough things to deal with.

You'll need to do some soul searching. If even a small bell rings for you...search and examine. It may be painful, but if you're willing to improve then you can make tremendous gains in your career.

Take some time to lick your wounds, pick up the lessons you need to learn, and get to work. You do have a lot to offer; your contributions can be of tremendous value. They just aren't hitting the mark right now.

Figure out why, adjust, and you can be that sought-out advisor. Pay attention to others who are being asked for their input. What are the valuable components of their advice? Are they centering on the people and offering new perspectives that others find valuable? Do they offer unique knowledge that helps the discussions, finances, or processes? Maybe they know more about your product than anyone else. Maybe they understand the customer channels like the back of their hand. They are offering something of value.

I see many professionals and leaders make the mistake of trying to offer something of value by inserting themselves.

They figure if they add value, they will be valuable. But if your intentions are off, everyone will know. You'll not be valued for your input; you'll be tolerated when you talk. They will move past you quickly. This is the opposite of what you're going for. Your ambition is in your way.

Worried that this might describe you sometimes? It's ok. You're human.

Let's take a deeper look. Do any of the following describe you?

Do you look for opportunities in the discussion to interject something brilliant?

Do you think about who else is on the call/in the room that you want to impress?

Do you think that you must speak during every meeting regardless of your role in that conversation?

Do you put value on talking during meetings because it gets you noticed?

I've met many women leaders who've been advised to always speak up in meetings and take every opportunity to prove themselves in front of their bosses. Maybe you, too, have received this advice at some point in your career. The intent of this advice is to push you out of your comfort zone and speak up, but it can be terrible advice if what you have to say isn't adding value to the discussion. I encourage you to speak up in general too, but don't speak just to talk... you should be contributing something. So, if you find yourself in the room and have something you want to say that adds to the conversation, great. If you find yourself looking for opportunities to wedge something in, get a word in, speak to be heard... you're focused on the wrong thing.

Shift your focus. If you want to impress others more than you want to add value, it will be obvious. Again, humans are innately aware creatures. Be honest with yourself here. No one wants to admit out loud that they jump into discussions to make themselves look good, but the truth is that everyone has done this at some point. It's more common when you just start a new job, just start a new career, or join a new group. You want to impress them. It's understandable, but it's the wrong way to go about it. Lead with your whole self. That means being honest with what you add to the discussion. Don't talk to be heard, talk to add value with no expectations for returns.

Signal #6: TEAM MEETINGS

Team meetings can tell you a lot about your leadership. I've had teams that are so comfortable it felt more like a family dinner than a team meeting. I've also had teams that were just getting to know each other and it felt a little awkward at first.

Another signal to watch for is how your team meetings go. If you pay attention...your team meetings will tell you everything you need to know about your team culture. Your meeting atmosphere is a symptom of how your team feels about you. You need to be engaging with your team.

Assuming you're not doing all of the talking in the meeting, how does your team engage? Do you have to work hard to get them to participate? Are there pregnant pauses when you ask questions? Or is the conversation comfortable and easy? Do team members easily interact with each other as well?

I hope you've had the opportunity to be a member of a team where there is easy flow of communication and a visible comradery. You will know it when you feel it.

If your team is comfortable with you there will be easy banter as the meeting is beginning, natural conversation flows throughout the meeting and it will just be comfortable. If this does not describe your team meetings, take a closer look. You can ignore the signs, but no one else in the room is ignoring them.

You set the tone for your team meetings. If they are uncomfortable or strained, you are responsible to fix it. Explore what you do or have done that limits the discussion. This is about fixing what YOU are doing that's creating that uncomfortable space. This one is difficult to correct once you've created it. If most of your meetings are uncomfortable, you've created a culture where people don't want to engage. Why is that? What have prior discussions looked like that created this culture?

So much of building your leadership skills will be about reflecting on how you need to change. This is one more reason it's so important to accept your experiences no matter how difficult and bring your whole self to your team. When you are playing a part as a leader, trying to impress or worried about making mistakes all the time.... you will come across as inauthentic. You won't let your guard down so your team won't either.

If your team meetings are feeling this way, you'll need to work on creating a safe space for people to feel more comfortable. This will start with building relationships and trust. You might consider getting your team together for an afternoon retreat with the intention to get to know each other better and discuss what you all want for your team going forward. This requires you to be vulnerable and authentic. This means you can't ask them to talk about themselves and then spend the whole time talking. You need to be able to open the space for real conversation. You do need to share something of yourself but don't present it to them. There are many team exercises that you can do that can guide this kind of conversation. Pick one and go for it.

Instead of scheduling an entire retreat, you could just open up the conversation with your team, telling them you'd like to have more interaction in your team meetings. Converse with them and be clear about what you'd like for your team. You might say, "I would like for our teams to get to know each other better and feel more comfortable sharing openly in our team meetings." Then ask your team, "how should we go about creating a safe space?"

After you ask that question, just listen!!! This is not your time to talk. You should shelter your opinion to make room for your team members to offer their thoughts. If you immedi-

ately counter anything they add, you will shut down the interactions.

Give yourself some grace as you navigate this space. The team
meeting has a culture that was built over time and past experiences. It won't be corrected in one conversation. It will take
time and repeated experiences to prove to your team that it
really is ok to be themselves in your team meetings. And
should you have a set-back or interaction that puts your team
back in that uncomfortable space, acknowledge the setback
and continue working to recover the gains you've made. Work
on this every time you meet and expect that it's going to take
many months to correct.

But know that this work you're doing with your team is totally
worth it. Not only will your teams respond, they'll be more
productive and effective. And you'll enjoy your work much
more when you're not always putting on a face. Some of my
most enjoyable experiences in my career have been with my
teams and particularly fun team meetings. These became my
people. I loved working with my teams. They felt like family
after a while. That gave me so much joy. I want that for
you too!

So, let's recap the signals...

#1 You're exhausted trying to have it all

#2 Listening to yourself talk

#3 What kinds of questions do you ask

#4 How you spend one on one time

#5 Are you asked for your input

#6 Team meetings

Do any of these signals ring a bell for you? Even if it's the tiniest bell. No one wants to admit to any of them, but please take a moment. I believe that even the best leaders fall into these traps at times. We are human, we can't be on the top of our game all the time. When my world was falling apart at home, when I couldn't think of anything but fear for my son, I was not a great leader. I was struggling and fell down on the job. I'm not asking you to accept defeat, I'm asking you to figure out the things you need to work on. When you work on those things you can grow into the amazing leader you are fully capable of becoming.

Accept that we are not perfect, and all leaders will slip. Sometimes we'll slip back into bad behaviors or self-doubts that have lingered since childhood. Sometimes we'll slip when our worlds are falling apart at home. Sometimes we'll slip because we've lost our passion for this work, and it's time to rediscover ourselves.

I keep these six signals on a sticky note right next to my mousepad on my desk as a reminder to myself. Not to beat myself up or be overly critical, but to remind myself that these are the pitfalls that I want to watch for and avoid. If I start to see these signals in myself, I course-correct quickly. For me that usually means self-reflection and then self-development and self-care. Over my career I've been a great leader, but that doesn't mean I never fell prey to any issues or ignored signals that were in front of me. In fact, I've fallen in the face of all of them. But I recognized the signals before they did too much damage to my team, my reputation, or to my self-confidence. And over time I built a reputation as the people's leader and I confidently built my career. You can do the same. It's not about knowing it all, having all the educational degrees, and never making a mistake. It's about knowing yourself, watching for signals, accepting input, and working to be better tomorrow than you were today. Every day.

5

CHECK YOURSELF

Keeping in mind the signals in the previous chapter now it's time to check yourself. When you recognize these signals the information you gain is golden. I want you to put your new wisdom to the test, particularly if you found yourself justifying why any of the signals have a different meaning for you. Maybe you heard a little bell go off, but quickly told yourself a story for why that didn't apply to you.

Now that you're observing, it's time to go deeper. You need to really listen to everything, verbal and especially non-verbal. Look for the signals, but do NOT respond to them. Take one week, look, listen, and think. Get yourself a journal that makes you feel badass and you can easily keep close to you. You are going to use this journal to write down your experiences. Have some fun with it, pick up a crazy colored notebook! Write about what happens, what happened before and after and how it made you feel. If your emotions bring up old wounds, write about those too. Journal your experiences without judgement. You might feel frustration, anger, disappointment as you really pay attention to the behaviors of others. This is about understanding the actions you take or don't take that impact the lives of those you lead. What can you learn from your team's behavior and actions that can help you learn about yourself? Only when you can be open to examining your talents and faults, can you start to improve.

Observe your team's interactions. Take into account the maturity stage of your team. Are you a brand-new team or an established team? Do you have new team members into an already close team?

And what is your stage as a leader? When you first take a new leader post, there are stages you'll go through with your teams and those you work most closely with. The stage you're at will affect your team interactions.

Stage One – CHECKING YOU OUT

Have you noticed that when you first started team members were engaging and interacted with you often, but now that's changed? People will give you the benefit of the doubt when you first start a job, even if you come with a poor reputation. They will usually give you a chance. But you have a short window before things change. Don't assume that because your first couple of team interactions were good that you are golden. This is work that builds on itself or breaks down. It's very true that when employees stop engaging there is something wrong.

Stage Two – FIRST FEW IMPRESSIONS

At stage two, your teams have had a few experiences with you. You've had the opportunity to set the tone for your team. At this point your team has already created an impression of you. They may be seeing some red flags if you've fallen into any of the traps discussed in the last chapter, or they may be impressed. Maybe you've handled the first few meetings well, and they are starting to trust and respect you. Either way it's early; they are still confirming their impressions.

Stage Three – IMPRESSIONS SET

At this point the team has likely solidified their impressions of you . They are not watching for anything different but expect you to be the leader that you've already demonstrated to them – good or bad.

Observe your team interactions but consider what stage you're at. Watch for signals and journal what you see. If you are an established leader, the team's interactions will likely be more comfortable, but the signals will be more subtle. Early teams will likely feel a little more awkward, signals should be easier to spot. When you're established with the team they have learned to adjust their behaviors to what they expect from you, so it will be more difficult to see the signals. The signals are still there, but you'll need to watch closer for them.

As you take the time to observe and journal, I urge you to be self-reflective, but don't beat yourself up. This activity sometimes allows our own self-doubt to creep in. While that's normal when we are acknowledging our weaknesses and mistakes, I don't want you to expend energy on your doubt. Here's the thing.... The act of acknowledging your faults is the greatest strength you can have as a leader. You can't improve yourself and be a better leader every day if you don't acknowledge faults. So, don't think about this as a pity party where you're going to beat yourself up and convince yourself you're not cut out for leadership.

Self-reflection, reading this book and doing the journal exercises tells me that you are willing to do the work that makes you cut out for this. Unlike you, there are many leaders whose egos can't handle this brutally honest self-reflection. They protect their feelings above all else, and instead of growing their leadership skills, they stagnate. They don't work on themselves; they just pretend that they are great.

But you're a different kind of leader. You really want to make your mark and positively impact all of those around you. You can't do that without pulling off the covers, taking a look at what's been hiding, and sorting it all out to improve your skills. So be proud of yourself! This is the hard stuff that too many leaders won't do. You are already showing your greatness, by delving into these chapters, laying out your weaknesses in a journal, and working your ass off to get better.

SO, NOW WHAT?

At this point you may be asking yourself what are you going to do with the new self discoveries you're making. As you consider the signals around you, you might be noticing a few things, but nothing earth shattering. Maybe you are connecting well with your team and your intuition guides you well, but you still feel like there are gaps in your leadership skills. If you're early in your career you may just be lacking experience. Maybe you've got some experience but you're not progressing like you envisioned. You might be at a point in your career, regardless of your years of experience, where you once loved what you do but have lost that spark. You want to be excited about work again. You want to rediscover joy and fulfillment from your career.

The first thing I ask my coaching clients to do is to dream again. Sit in silence and really dream. I like to sit in nature, go for a walk or find a peaceful setting where I won't be distracted. Sometimes I'll go for a drive to think. I want you to journal about your ideal day. Not just a work day but your entire life. What are things you really want from your life? What do you value? How do you enjoy spending your time? What gives you energy?

In the next chapters we'll talk about some of the things you'll need to know and do to be a great leader and to love your career and your life. Dreaming helps lay out a strategic vision, but without those innermost hopes of yours journaled, the focus becomes tactical. If you aren't completely authentic in your actions, you'll move farther away from your strategic vision. Only when you are your whole, true self will you truly be happy. I can tell you what the best leaders do, even how they behave/their actions, but only you can determine your leadership approach. HOW do you want to lead? As you consider the advice in this book, always do so by aligning the advice with the kind of leader you want to be. Your leadership identity starts with your values. The things you value set your leadership foundation. So, take the time to really understand what you value.

Many of us get to a point in our career when we realize that we've lost ourselves a little bit. When I was 25, I was an ambitious, driven, force of nature. I was a young mother and an up-and-coming leader. I was smart and sassy, the life of the party and the work team. I knew I wanted to lead, but I didn't know what, or who, I wanted to lead. At that time, my dreams had less to do with a specific company or industry; I just knew that I wanted to be in charge and do big things. It really was that simple. In my dreams I dreamt of being CEO of my own company, running someone else's company or leading a huge non-profit organization. At the heart of my dreams were my values. I wanted to have significant decision-making authority, and whatever I did, I needed to make a positive difference in the world. Looking back now, I can see how my dreams and values aligned, but if you'd asked me at that time, I wouldn't have thought I was clear on my values and my goals. I was just a dreamer.

The thing with dreamers is that we'll keep going, excited about our future, but with no real path. That totally described me earlier in my career!

I had been going through my career, buzzing from one thing to the next, driven by the excitement of the new thing. I had some amazing experiences, but before I knew it, I was in my late 30's and had lost my dream. It seemed like it had slipped out of my hands somehow. I was approaching mid-career, and I felt lost and stuck.

This was at the same time when my son attempted suicide. I remember sitting in the hospital room. He had just been brought in by ambulance. I was numb. The next 12 hours were a blur. It felt like everything was in slow motion but happened in a few blinks of an eye. It's hard to explain.

Later that night I sat next to his hospital bed. He was sleeping peacefully and gently holding my hand. I was a shell of a woman. I was pale and exhausted. I laid my forehead on the bed next to him and just breathed. Time stood still. I was so grateful that he was alive, but I was lost.

Then something stirred in me. That was the night that I decided my life needed to change. I got angry...really pissed. I was angry at my circumstances, angry at God, and angry at my boss. I had to sift through all that anger to figure out what I needed next.

What I found was I needed to get back to my core values. My foundational value is authenticity. I don't want to pretend to be anyone that I'm not. I don't want to put on a pretty face and tell a great story if that's not the truth. I want to be unapologetically me. And I realized that I hadn't been doing any of that. I was hurting, my kids were hurting, and my marriage was suffering. I decided in that hospital room that I was not accepting anything in my life that wasn't completely real. From that day on, I started making some big changes. It took months, even years for some of those changes to stick, but that is the secret to my joy now. My son's experience taught me that I don't want to regret anything.

You are reading this book for a reason, and you also have a story. Explore what is important to you and what changes you might need to make to live up to your values.

As you review the practical advice for your leadership approach, consider it all from the standpoint of what you value...and make it your own.

6

SETTING GOALS ISN'T ENOUGH. SET CLARITY TOO

Y ou have big ideas and a big vision for your career. You also have big dreams for your teams when you are a leader. As you lead others, you'll be setting a vision and a plan for them and your organization. As you lay out these ideas and plans, they all seem very clear to you, but might not easily land with your team. Many leaders are frustrated as they try to extend their vision to their teams. It's not as simple as telling them where you're going, and it all just magically works. The truth is, it takes a lot of energy to lead others to follow you. You'll need to inspire them to follow your vision.

A lot of leaders make the mistake of assuming that their teams see their vision the same way they do. At some point, most leaders will confuse their teams. We expect that we will be clear; our vision will make sense to everyone. It won't take much explanation at all...they will just "get it." That's easy, right? Um...wrong!

Setting goals can be tricky, and many leaders don't set really clear, specific goals. As a leader, you really do need to take the time to assess your team, your market, and your business strengths and weaknesses. Engage your team to get their perspectives on what goals will be most important for your success.

Many teams find tremendous value by holding an annual planning retreat to work through the plan and set goals.

Once you've decided on your key goals, over communicate. Write them down, put them on your wall, and make sure you and your team can see them every day. Tie your regular team communication to your goals. Find the right cadence to tie back your regular operational and project updates.

Now that you have set clear goals how do you keep your teams focused? Most of the time teams, with the best of intentions, will find themselves facing daily challenges that naturally draw their attention away. There is no doubt you need to tend to the daily demands of your business. It's the foundation of your service level no matter your industry. But when you find yourself at the end of every day or every week, and you can't say what you've done to work towards your goals, you are too distracted.

All leaders will get distracted. Good leaders will eventually recognize that their teams are distracted; great leaders will recognize it early. When I was working in Healthcare during the COVID pandemic, it was natural for healthcare organizations to respond swiftly. It was, in fact, necessary. But parts of the business were less impacted than others. The foundational goals of some departments did not change. They still held true and in fact became more critical for contributing to the overall health of the organization.

But distractions surrounded the teams. The teams were tremendously busy answering the needs of the pandemic, communicating often with each other to maintain connected-ness and working on less valuable items. This made it difficult to focus on the overall strategic goals. The urgent items were overall less valuable to the health of the organization, but take a lot of time, leaving less time to focus on the important strategic goals.

Those less-valuable items are sometimes referred to as the "noise" of the day. The things that you probably need to let go. You've checked the necessary boxes to show you've completed them, but does this work really add value to your business?

We've all had those leaders who ask for reports, spreadsheets, analysis that they never do anything with. Before you ask for another spreadsheet, understand what you plan to do with the information. If you are giving direction to complete a task with no real intention of value-add, you may be contributing to the noise. Just be aware of these requests. All leaders will get distracted. My best advice is to ask yourself at the end of every day what you've done towards your main goals. It's normal to have days that you don't contribute to the overall goal, but you should have more days working towards your goals than not.

7

LEARNING TO MAKE GOOD DECISIONS

Our life is a series of moments and decisions. You can predict the likely trajectory of your life based on the decisions you make. The way you do one thing is the way you do all things, so learning to make good decisions is a skill that will make your life infinitely better. One of the key skills of any leader is the ability to make good decisions. This doesn't mean that you always make the right decision, in fact you will make mistakes. We're human, and many people don't want to admit to a bad decision. This is a missed opportunity. Rather than dismiss mistakes by deflecting them on others, take each as a lesson.

Please, don't convince yourself that you're making good decisions if you're not. Look for the signals we've discussed; they can also help you determine if your decision-making game needs help. If you are having multiple failures, be that strategic or operational goals or project failures, take note.

Every failure should be assessed for lessons to be learned. Is there a common theme in the failures? What could have been done differently? Pay particular attention to the decision points, and play out what could have been different.

I remember when I was leading our local YMCA and made a big decision that turned out to be wrong. We were facing a difficult financial challenge when a major source of funding was cut off. We needed to make some changes to our program and membership model, including pricing changes. I collected lots of input, engaged our national organization and our board of directors, and collaborated with my leadership team. We needed to change our pricing model and adjust our marketing strategy. It was a costly change. I led the decision to adjust our model. Though many contributed to the process, I was responsible for the decision.

I remember being so confident in the plan. I was young and inexperienced. But I was also smart and had engaged all the right people to ensure I was confident in our approach. We made all the changes and embarked on a difficult year of not seeing results. As the weeks and months passed and we didn't see the financial upswing we had hoped for, I wanted to crawl in a corner. I was so embarrassed! Doubts crept in, and I started telling myself that I wasn't cut out for this kind of work. My self-talk was cruel at times. I went through a tough time in my life and career during these months.

But I didn't stay there. I accepted that we were not seeing the outcomes we wanted and took an objective look at the situation. I set aside my emotions and dropped my doubts; with a clear head and vision, I was able to assess the decisions I'd made along the way. I could see where different decisions would have resulted in different outcomes, but I could also see a lot of factors that were not in my control. I could see where things went wrong, and I learned valuable lessons that allowed me to let go of my doubts. I was able to push forward confidently, not because I would never make another mistake, but because I knew that I could learn and move on from them.

This was the biggest 'mistake' of my career if measured by the number of people impacted. I was able to recover from this and get better as my career advanced. If I can get past this, you can get past your mistakes, too.

If you do make a bad decision, own up to it. I once had a leader who made many questionable decisions. It was common for her mistakes to be visible, and as all engaged teams do... they would ask her about it. Her go-to response was always to explain why she made the decision and state that she was not wrong; the circumstances had adjusted in some way. In fact, she didn't ever think she was wrong. She took a lot of time to explain herself to the teams, when all they really needed to hear was that she made a mistake.

Don't let your ego get in your way. This response is common in leaders who are very concerned about how they look. We all have an ego. I don't fault you for that. But if you want to be a great leader you need to not care so much about yourself. I know this seems counter to what naturally appears to make sense. Being the best for others will allow you to grow into the best version of yourself as a leader, which in turn will make you look good. Really good. Put your team before you...period.

With the drive to want to do well for your teams you may find yourself afraid to make the tough decisions. Or any decisions. Don't make the mistake of hesitating too long to make decisions. Sometimes leaders can be so risk averse that they spend too much time assessing the situation before they will make decisions. It's a talent to know when to make the decisions. Some leaders act too quickly without good information or acting on emotion/impulse. Some leaders act too slowly wanting to collect more information. The leader that acts too quickly is seen as ill informed, out of touch and impulsive. The leader that acts too slowly can be considered indecisive and unhelpful. Of course, hindsight is always 20/20 and everyone will be a "Monday morning quarterback", but over time you should be able to see a trend in your leadership approach. If you're not sure whether you're perceived as too slow or too quick, ask your teams or your peers for feedback. Over time, knowing when to make the decision will get easier, more intuitive. The best lesson here is to ensure you have enough information, without overanalyzing, to make a good decision at the time. You might still make a mistake, but if you do it with the best of intentions and good information you'll bounce back.

Though it's incredibly frustrating to work with leaders who make impulsive decisions, I would much prefer them over the leader that won't make decisions. The indecisive leader is not doing his/her job. Don't expect to stay in leadership roles very long if you are uncomfortable making decisions. It's fairly common for individual contributors to get promoted into leadership roles where they find themselves way out of their comfort zone. it's necessary to go out of your comfort zone to grow, but if you get too far out, you might become paralyzed. In this situation you won't grow, and you might take a big blow to your reputation, ego, and self-worth. I firmly believe that everyone should do the things they love and that make them shine. If leadership doesn't feel like that for you, go find yourself again.

8

APPRECIATE DIFFERENCES

It's difficult to have deep meaningful relationships with every member of your team enough that you can always know what's going on in their lives. But it's important to try to understand your team members as individuals. They each have a perspective that's unique to them. They will see things differently than you. Pay attention to the information around you and what is shared with you. This information, when used with compassion and understanding, will help you be a better leader.

Let me explain with a story... Julie has a large team of about 50 people. About 40 of them report to line managers, who then report to Julie. It's reasonable that Julie is not closely-acquainted with each team member. The team had experienced a heartbreaking accident in their community that resulted in the death of a family many knew personally. The teams were emotional and grieving. Julie preferred not to talk about "what happens outside of work," so she declined her line managers' advice about adding the topic to the all-team meeting.

Inevitably, the team asked Julie about the accident at the meeting. She was not prepared to open the conversation and minimized the importance by brushing it off and changing the topic. This, of course, frustrated her team. They were angry. The managers reporting to Julie did damage control for the next several weeks, but Julie's reputation never recovered.

Julie did not take into account the environment where her team lived and worked. She was not impacted personally by the tragedy, and she hadn't emotionally responded in the same way as her team. Her mistake was that she believed her emotions were the same as everyone else had been experiencing. Because she wasn't emotional about the situation, she didn't understand why anyone on her team should let it impact their work.

There is a lot to consider when you have trouble understanding others' perspectives. The best leaders not only accept others but appreciate their differences and gain value from those differences. As a leader you'll need to check your own experiences and be sure to not apply your expectations to everyone. The way you see the world is going to be different from others. Understanding that just because someone has a different response to a situation than you would, does not make that person wrong.

In Julie's case, this event was not the only time the team had questioned Julie's leadership. But it was the last time they gave her the benefit of the doubt. This was the final straw for some of them. In the next 12 months they lost 15% of their staff to turnover. I'm not saying that we can directly attribute that turnover to that one event, but it certainly didn't help anything.

The best thing you can do as leaders when it comes to understanding people is to be aware of your biases. We all have biases. As leaders we should know our biases and constantly be checking them. If we regularly ask ourselves "does my approach change if I look at this a different way?" we can hope to make better decisions.

9

SETTING REALISTIC EXPECTATIONS

Have you ever had a leader who expected you to be at their beck and call? How about the leader that acts like you'd stabbed them in the back because you considered interviewing for another job? Or the leader who doesn't give a crap about your Mom being sick or personal challenges you have at home?

While I accept that years ago perhaps these expectations were more normal, they absolutely are NOT today. If you find yourself questioning the "commitment" of your team members because they have a life outside of work, I want you to think about why you feel that way.

I once had a leader who had extremely unrealistic expectations. In his opinion, the work was your first priority, always. You could have a personal life, but only when he didn't need you. He would text and email at all hours of the day and night.

If you did not respond quickly, within an hour, you were questioned about your commitment. Appointments during the work-day were not appreciated. He would question you about why you couldn't do that on "your own time." He was a tyrant that I left as soon as I could secure another job. When I told him I was leaving, he acted like I had stabbed him in the back. And the next day, he acted like I was invisible. He was awful, and I was glad to be rid of him.

On another occasion, I worked as a peer to a leader who followed a similar approach to the tyrant. She was often found reminding her team that they had to "earn their stripes." It didn't matter how much value they added; it only mattered how committed they were and how long they stayed in the job. She berated people for volunteering outside of work or having family obligations. She explained to her team that the job should always be their first priority and anything else they chose to do would reflect poorly on their advancement opportunities. It's safe to say no one wanted to report to her.

Not only is the world changing, but the workforce is changing, too. You do not own your employees' time. You hire them to do a job, they do it well, and you pay them. If you want commitment, loyalty, engagement, and longevity, you need to treat them well. Treating them like a product you own is not going to do that.

I believe that the workforce of the future is going to continue to evolve. As leaders, we need to change with it. We need to be able to accept working styles that are different from your own. We need to be able to look at the work-day with increasing flexibility. How can we create a work environment that will attract talented teams and encourage engagement?

I'm so tired of hearing more seasoned leaders talk about these "lazy" young people. Everyone has incredible value. I'm proud to have had the pleasure to lead a tremendously diverse group of individuals. They all taught me something that I've taken with me. I'm encouraged that the workplace is adjusting to allow for more flexible options so we can benefit from everyone's talents. The "young people" have got some things figured out that my father did not understand until an injury put him in early retirement. We do not live for work.... we work and live and love and travel and enjoy each other's company.

Let's take a minute here to acknowledge that if you are truly authentic with yourself and those around you, you should be able to accept your own experiences and that of others merely as information. Don't place judgement on the information or on those who have different beliefs than you do. You wouldn't want that judgement placed on you.

Bottom-line, treat people well.

10

EMBRACE AUTHENTICITY

O ver the years I've learned so much from all the mistakes I've made and all the silly things I've watched others do. I've read a lot of leadership "self-help" books that don't really tell you the down and dirty shit. I hope you took some wisdom from these tell-all examples and related tips that will help you avoid these same mistakes. Now that you know the mistakes, let's focus on the positives.

Before we move on, I want to say that if you felt like you had anything in common with the examples or issues noted in the previous chapters, I'm glad you're here with me on Chapter 10. I had a lot to share, and if you felt a little self-conscious or just plain bad about yourself, don't. That was not my intention.

Remember, every great leader got that way because they've made many, many mistakes. They learned from them and got better. Over time they made fewer mistakes. Leaders don't ever stop making mistakes; it comes with being human! So, give yourself some grace.

Ok, so now that you can accept that you're not perfect, let's work on what we really need to do....build you up!

Every leader has one common problem: at times they do not believe they are worthy of the job. They don't always admit it but trust me... every leader feels like an imposter sometimes. Some mistakes even happen because the leader is trying so hard to feel worthy.

There are many occasions in life when we try too hard. Sometimes we try too hard and push people away. Sometimes, we're in a relationship that just doesn't work, but we keep going through the motions and pushing for something that's not there. What about the friendships that we try so hard for... where we come off like a stalker! The project that we over-engineer by trying to impress the boss, but it ends up backfiring because they think we can't cut through the noise and communicate succinctly.

Ironically, in leadership you are more credible and trusted when you are authentic, genuine, and can be vulnerable. You may be trying to build a leader persona of the strong, decisive, courageous leader. You can be all those things, but they just might mean something a little different than you think.

If you think a strong leader never breaks a sweat, is never wrong, and always has the right answer, then you will be disappointed. Change your story.

A strong leader is someone you respect, generally like (not a requirement, but high acceptance ratings), and trust to do the right thing. How can you feel that way about another human being if they are always putting on a false front?

You can't truly get to know someone like that.

Conversely, if a leader is authentic, is "real" with you, sharing information as they can and showing you who they are as a person, you are more likely to trust them. If you always put on a persona, you aren't authentic, and others will think you have something to hide.

You don't have to be perfect; you will gain more credibility when you are courageous enough to be authentic, especially in times of crisis. This doesn't mean falling apart emotionally or that you can afford to be indecisive. However, when you are genuine as a person first and accept that you can't be a different person when you're leading, you will more readily be seen as a great leader.

WORK ON YOU

This book is not really about leadership. I know, I probably should have told you earlier. ☺

It's about being the best YOU so that you can be the best leader, friend, spouse, parent you can be. This book is about so much more than leadership. There are signals in every aspect of your life like the ones at your work. My greatest hope for you is that you were able to find something in these pages that you can relate to. Something that you can admit to yourself that is not at its best. Because that means you are ready. It's time to work on you.

11

TAKING RESPONSIBILITY

I grew up on a farm in rural Minnesota. We had a small herd of dairy cattle and a very big, beautiful red barn...just like in the movies. One day while my parents were milking, I was playing in the barn. I remember distinctly that I was playing house and pretending that I had a huge pot of stew. I need a spoon to stir the stew! Mind you, this was all make believe. BUT for some reason the spoon had to be real. There was a metal 'spoon' sticking out of the ground. Perfect! But it was stuck in the ground. So what does a tenacious, resourceful little girl do? Break it off, and pull it out.

It turns out that the 'spoon' was a natural gas line into the barn. While I stirred my imaginary stew, the gas slowly filled the barn, and within its walls were my Mom and 20 head of cattle. Fortunately, I smelled the gas and knew something was wrong. I alerted my Mother, and she promptly shut off the gas and cleared the barn. No one was hurt other than my parent's pocketbook for the repair.

After the gas cleared, my Dad was quite insistent that he understand what happened. You see, I am the oldest of four children. I am the 'responsible' one. I was also the in-charge sister that ruled our little gang. I had managed to alert my Mother of the danger without taking any responsibility. I mean, zero responsibility. Sweet little angel here, just saving the world. It certainly wasn't MY fault.

I had never lied like that before. I was terrified. This set the stage for one of the most defining situations in my childhood.

This story takes place in a time when spanking your children was common practice. As my father proceeded to interrogate the four of us, no one admitted to any wrongdoing. Of course, they didn't admit to it; they did nothing wrong. I was alone in this criminal activity. They didn't even know that I was the one who had done it!

Throughout the interrogation, I maintained my innocence. I told myself, and everyone around me, that I didn't do it! My father extended a round of spankings to our bottoms and asked the four of us kids to talk it out. He wanted a suspect! After a couple of rounds of spankings, I managed to convince my brother to take the blame. The interrogation was over, but my brother was in a LOT of trouble. He had extra chores for a long time. I felt horrible. But not enough to admit it!

That afternoon our bottoms were stinging. The next day I told my friends at school about my sore bottom. Turns out they told my teacher, who called the principal, who asked me some very uncomfortable questions about the nature of the punishment. I didn't understand the consequence of the school asking these questions. I was a child. But the school called in my parents. I was appalled and even further embarrassed.

I had almost blown up the barn. I had lied. I had convinced an innocent to take the blame. I had inadvertently gotten the school involved. It was a hot mess.

And I still did not admit what I did.

In fact, it would be over a year later while at a church retreat. I had my first truly spiritual experience at this retreat, cried like a baby, and admitted everything to my father.

He laughed!!

He squeezed my shoulder, his easy touch of kindness, and he said it was OK. Just like that! He forgave me without question. That day I learned the beauty of peace and forgiveness. I felt that release of letting go of what burdens you.

I had lived that year with a secret. It had slowly eroded me. I was taking a lot of energy to hide that secret and live with the guilt. What if I had taken responsibility from the beginning? I couldn't start to move past it, and I couldn't grow from the experience, until I accepted full responsibility.

I tell you this story because we all have things in our lives that we give more energy to than we probably should. How much time and energy do you spend on things in your life that would be different if you took responsibility. This goes far beyond those things that you did wrong, those actions you feel guilty for doing. Taking responsibility for your life means not only taking responsibility for your actions but for your thoughts as well. Taking responsibility means you accept your whole self. It is in some ways the most vulnerable place you can put yourself. To truly own the things you did, the pain you've inflicted, the awful things you tell yourself deep in your psyche. We all have those negative thoughts about ourselves. Some accept those as truth, and some shove them down and ignore them. I'm suggesting you take those thoughts on with all your force. When you do that you can grow and gain greater abundance and happiness in your life.

So, what's your barn story?

Or addiction story?

Or story of loss?

Think about those situations in your life that permanently cemented a value into your very heart. All the things you put the greatest value in come from what you've been taught, either through well-meaning parents or a significant experience. You may be taught the value of hard work by watching your parents build a business or commit their lives to the military. You may have a deep-seated belief that you are limited in some way; for instance, women used to be taught through societal norms that they are not good at math. Relationships are often rooted in how you were treated as you grew up. Everyone has their own stories, sometimes awful stories, that make us who we are. And the learning just keeps coming with every new "gut punch" that life serves us. Because, yes, bad things will happen in your life.

12

EVERYONE HAS THEIR OWN STORY

I find some peace in knowing that everyone has a story. In fact, once I accepted that my own story was not really that unique, I felt such freedom! All too often, we carry shame because of our stories. That shame can be debilitating. Sometimes, it's the shame that alters our behavior more than the things that actually happened. I'm not minimizing trauma. Human beings are subjected to some very disturbing circumstances. Those traumas are very real. How each person lives after trauma and the choices they make in the future can continue the trauma or allow healing to come from it.

You might be asking yourself what this has to do with leadership.

Everything!!

All the signals we've talked about are actual behaviors that you can redirect, but they are indeed behaviors. Most of us act without thinking much about it. Our first reaction is the most true representation of us. Your behaviors are those instinctive reactions. As a leader you are still a person. You are likely to lean into your instincts first. Many of the issues we've talked about happen because leaders lean into their first instincts. It is possible to adjust from your first instinct and respond in a healthier way. The best leaders are not free from trauma. Again...everyone, even great leaders, has their own story!

To be at your best, you need to be able to understand your own limitations. That means understanding your own traumas and the deep-seated beliefs that limit you. It's critical to work through your past, your difficult circumstances, and really understand yourself.

Let me tell you the story of Tammi, a senior level leader. Tammi had a deep-seated need for approval, particularly by authority figures. She believed in following orders, no questions asked. There is a time and place for command and control leadership, in military operations for example. But most organizations do not need, nor do they benefit from, command and control leadership. It can be effective in times of crisis and short term, but rarely long term and only in specific cultures. Those cultures will not attract the vast majority of employees that you need to succeed in an ever changing, diverse world.

In Tammi's case she did not understand her own biases toward authority figures and command and control approaches. She just assumed that this was the best way to lead, and everyone should fall in line with her. A typical blind spot of command and control leaders. My way or the highway.

When she couldn't see the value of other approaches, she didn't look any further at her own strengths and weaknesses. Her command and control approach frustrated those who worked for her. It contributed to turnover on the team and caused difficulty recruiting talented employees. But her need to please authority figures was far more damaging than she realized. She was so concerned about what her boss would think that she didn't think for herself. She certainly would never question him, and she blindly led her team into troubled waters.

Here's the thing, her team all saw this weakness in her. They were left with very little confidence in her. After all, she didn't think for herself; she only parroted what her boss said. And when her boss didn't have all the information, she failed to inform him for fear of his disapproval. In short, she was not doing her job, but she thought she was doing a great job. As long as her boss was happy, she was great. It didn't matter what anyone on her team thought because they had no authority over her. They were considered to have less value to her. So, what happens? She gets moved around the organization as teams get fed up with her. She damages every team she touches. And she still thinks she's great.

This story makes me so sad. I never want to be blind to my weaknesses. Unfortunately, as we move up in the organization, we often find that fewer and fewer people are comfortable being honest with you. What if they act like Tammi and won't even provide you with the information you need? How does that help you? It doesn't.

Don't be like Tammi, and don't hire Tammi. Neither situation is good for you as a leader.

But most importantly, learn from Tammi. Everyone has biases, including you. Consider those topics that make you feel uncomfortable, maybe even frustrated or angry. Those emotions are signals to you that something is off. It may help you recognize where you have bias. If you can't figure out your own biases, ask others whom you trust. When you recognize these areas of bias, you can do something with them.

When you've identified and accepted your own biases, you can start to evolve your thinking. In this way you can keep learning and improving your skills. More importantly, you will be a better person than you were before.

As you've probably figured out by now, the best leaders are really great people first. You can learn the tactical actions and core competencies to make good decisions as a leader. You can get a great education and continually learn the things you need to know to inform your decisions. But for now, let's stay focused on the tough stuff. The stuff that's not taught in a classroom. The real challenge of human existence is survival. I'm not talking about surviving like our early humans. The risk used to be the elements, starvation, wild animals. Now the risks come from other humans. We are not great to each other. As we work really hard to try to take care of loved ones, there are situations all around our world that create a variety of traumas in our lives. I told you the story of traumas in my life so far. There will be more to come. As I grow in my experience, I hope I'm better equipped when they do.

Everyone has experienced some kind of trauma. You carry those traumas with you. It might mean that you struggle to trust others. It might mean that you only feel valuable when you work 80-hour weeks. It might mean that you only feel secure when you have $100,000 in your savings account. No matter the trauma, you carry that baggage.

We are a society of increasing depression and anxiety. We face the day with ongoing stressors that manifest in a variety of ways. So, it's no longer a world of fearing the wild animals, but instead living in constant fear that we harbor from our traumas. We can survive trauma, but it takes work to thrive beyond it. This might seem like it has nothing to do with leadership, but I assure you it does. Everyone has trauma, and everyone has their own resulting story and experiences. Like Tammi, who harbored trauma from a strong military family who taught her for years to never question authority. She failed to see it, but it was there. Her upbringing conditioned her to feel fear, stress, and anxiety if she doesn't follow what she knows – respect authority at all costs. Her fear of disrespecting authority was so deeply rooted that she was not capable of finding other ways to interact with authority figures. Until she figures out how to do that, she won't be able to lead effectively.

So, what's your trauma? What has happened to you that defines who you are? What are those things that you believe without question? Those things that terrify you? Even if you never lead a team, if you can work through your traumas, you will live a much happier life and be a better person to all those who need you, whether they are your teams or your families or your communities.

Assuming you do want to be a great leader (that's why you picked up this book, right?) the first thing you need to do is take a good hard look at the things that scare you. The things that make you stressed. The times that you can't sleep, what's on your mind? Understand who you are and what makes you tick. Perhaps more importantly, what makes you frustrated, in a state when you are not at your best. You know it...that state when you misstep, say the wrong things, and generally piss people off. What happens right before that state? To be a great leader you need to understand all that makes you good and bad. Work to maximize the good stuff and minimize the bad. It's a simple concept, but it may be the hardest thing you ever do.

There is a good reason that our therapists & psychologists are overbooked in this country. We all are dealing with our own story. So, figure out what it is for you. Get a good therapist, spiritual healer, coach, or whatever works for you. I know a leader who stays grounded with a personal life coach who guides her through meditation, well-being, and source energy work. You may not believe in the same things, but it doesn't matter. It works for her. That's what matters. She's one of the most centered, happy people I know. Who the HELL cares how she finds her peace?!

It's a much bigger mistake to scoff at another for finding peace and continue your own miserable life without trying to get better. So, find your guide. Sit with your deep-seated values that are not serving you, and understand where they come from. Understand why you self-sabotage in these areas. Work on ways to respond more effectively that will keep you leading at your best. It will take time and continual work. You will forever be working on being your best person. No one will ever get to the ultimate destination in this regard.

You will always have more to learn, more to give, more to improve. Never stop. Continuous improvement efforts will make you a better person and increase your leadership abilities.

As you explore your own weaknesses and open yourself to continual self-improvement you'll find another benefit. Most people appreciate the leader who is "real." When you pretend that you don't have troubles like everyone else, others are less likely to relate to you. Why is that? Because everyone has their own shit. Yes, everyone!

I find great peace in this because that means I'm not alone. I don't want to measure my traumatic shit against yours or anyone else's. That's just not going to be healthy or productive. But when we understand that we all have these things in our lives that weigh on us, then we can begin to get past them, maybe in a more meaningful way than we would if we felt like we were alone.

So much of the western world is only now opening up to the idea of having conversations about the bad things that happen to us. We don't talk about abuse, loss, or that we've been victims of any kind of crime. The mental toll this has taken on our communities is significant. Stress continues to increase with faster moving technologies, social media, job expectations, schools becoming more complex, and pressures ever increasing across all of our lives, including our children's. It's no wonder that mental health diagnoses, including depression, anxiety, mood, and personality disorders are at an all-time high. The goodness in this is that we can expect that it's affecting every single person we know in one way or another, so why not pull the covers off and really talk about it?!

We are the product of our experiences. Some of us have had an easier time than others. Some have had terrible troubles. Either way, the life you've lived has made you the person you are today. I should say, the life you have lived *and your response to it*. As a leader, you need to be able to continually learn, grow, and improve yourself. To do that...you need to deal with your shit. Deal with those things that have happened to you; those things that have shaped you. Acknowledge that some of the shaping is not for the best. The alcoholic parent may have taught you to be super responsible, but it also may have left you distrustful and prone to succumb to alcoholism yourself. The military family taught you discipline and hard work, but you may not be the strongest leader when it comes to collaboration and innovative thinking. The tough neighborhood might have taught you to always watch your back and take care of those close to you but taught you to ignore injustice of others.

Any experience can be described with both negative and positive connotations. You can find the negative in anything or the positive in anything. Which do you look for?

Think about your experiences and the emotions, responses, and behaviors that you lean into first. Those are your stress responses, and they indicate the things that come most naturally to you. If those natural tendencies are not serving you well in leadership, you'll need to understand them and work to correct your behaviors. Don't work to forget the reasons you have those responses. The traumas you have experienced do not just go away. In fact, trying to bury them would inevitably lead to unpredictable behaviors when you least expect it. If you can work on addressing the source of your negative stress responses, you can work on correcting them. You will always have a natural stress response, but over time you can learn to recognize when it might happen and head it off at the pass. Then you are better prepared for a more predictable, appropriate response. As leaders you will make mistakes, but the more you can protect your teams from your negative stress responses the better.

So, what do you do if you haven't really addressed these things about you? Many seek therapy, which is highly recommended with significant traumas. Some work through strengths assessments and personality tests to better understand themselves. I recommend working with a trusted mentor, advisor, or leadership coach to help you understand the connection between how you feel and why you respond a certain way. All of these things can help you understand yourself and grow.

All too often, leaders dismiss this part of their development. They think it doesn't really matter what happened in the past. I find those who fight this will struggle the most with leadership development. I think that's got a lot to do with the ability to be self-reflective. Some clients will tell me they believe they are self-reflective, but when we start working together it becomes evident that they struggle to take in any constructive information. No one wants to hear what they need to work on, but that's the deal. Leaders are ever learning. If you can't take feedback you should not be in leadership. You will not be able to lead others. No one will follow you.

13

VULNERABILITY

So, assuming you really work on yourself, let's talk about how vulnerability can be a great gift to your teams. I know this is not comfortable. Brene Brown has done some tremendous work on vulnerability. Her TedTalk went viral in 2010. If you don't know Dr. Brown, please read her stuff!

Vulnerability is about having the courage to say and do the things that open you up to criticism. But you do it anyway. You open yourself up, and bring up topics or question others, even when it comes with some risk of what others will think of you. For example, when my son attempted suicide, I chose to be open about what had happened. I sent an email to my team with some level of detail (not everything) of what happened and what I needed from them, namely time and grace. I didn't expect to have retributions from this sharing, but it's not always comfortable for everyone. What happened after I opened up to the people in my life was so much greater than I ever imagined. I was welcomed with open arms, literally. I cried when I returned, and my teams surrounded me with strength and compassion. I had people reach out to me and thank me for being so open because they had their own experiences with mental illness that they didn't feel able to talk about openly. I was a leader. It was important to me to be open with colleagues because I wanted to lean on them, but more than that, I was setting an example that created a culture that made others feel more comfortable.

At the time I didn't think about how my vulnerability might contribute to my leadership; I was thinking about what I needed. I hate to say that, but it's true. In the end, I learned a valuable lesson about leading with vulnerability. That was the beginning of my journey to really understand that we need to take care of ourselves before we can take care of others. Leadership is all about taking care of others so they will take care of your business.

Another example of vulnerability, I have a client (Nicole) who found herself in a big work meeting. Her team was a large group of project managers. One of Nicole's project managers was presenting to the meeting. An executive of the company was in the meeting and raised some critical questions of her project manager. The questions were extremely critical and placed some blame on the project manager for lack of delivery. The room was charged emotionally with concern over failing to meet a big deadline that meant millions of dollars to the company. But the criticism of the project manager was not productive. Nicole was faced with a dilemma; if she supported her project manager, she would disagree with a very influential leader.

And that's when it happens. Take the risk and put yourself out there, or be quiet and do damage control with your team later. These are the moments that they don't teach you about. These are the moments when leaders really stand up. The reality is most leaders take a pause, second guess themselves, and don't say anything. The moment to speak up can pass fairly quickly. One moment it's there, then it's gone. It's a missed opportunity to be vulnerable and to do the right thing.

Nicole took her opportunity. She asked to speak. She made her way to the front of the room and grabbed a microphone. She did not attack or blame. She focused on thanking the project manager for his efforts and asking for stronger collaboration with the other project teams. She encouraged the attendees to talk about how they can improve the teamwork to meet the goals.

The influential leader who had made the critical comments was quieted. Other leaders were impressed. Most importantly the teams knew that she would focus on the right things, wouldn't place blame, and demonstrated strength in leadership to pull them all together.

What if her past experiences made her fear speaking up during moments of conflict, and her fear response was so strong that she just sat there when this all transpired? That's why it's important to know your stress responses.

All this goes back to really taking care of your traumas, taking care of your deficits, taking care of your emotions, and taking care of yourself!

You might be thinking.... I don't want to wait to deal with my shit before I take that promotion! I get it. That's fine. You can start to work on yourself right now. What are you going to do tomorrow to work on yourself?

When I meet with clients for the first time, I spend extra time getting to know what brought them to me, I ask them about the most important elements in their life, what questions make them uncomfortable, and what questions make them light up? I'm looking for the triggers that we need to work on. No kidding ....95% of the time the triggers are deeply rooted in past experiences. My first order of business is to help my client understand their responses to those experiences. That is where the breakthroughs start. You begin to learn and understand yourself better than ever before. You put your newfound wisdom into your work and into your leadership and you get better. Period.

Break through first, better leader next.

14

THE BEST LEADERS FOR OUR FUTURE

I truly believe that what we expect of our leaders has changed over the decades. One hundred years ago in the western world, our greatest leaders were strong and influential. Some of that influence came from financial resources. The strongest people with the greatest resources influenced the most. The industrial era showed us what those leaders could accomplish, and we came to recognize that as great leadership.

Seventy or so years later in the 1960-1980s, leaders needed to be smart. Sure a few got lucky and resources still carried some a long way, but you didn't lead very long if you didn't understand how the business worked. Finances, business savvy and technical intelligence was the price of admission for most leaders. Those aspiring into these roles were well educated and well read. You had to be smart to get noticed.

I believe that we are entering yet another era of leadership when intellect is needed, but the best leaders will lead with heart. Understanding the fundamentals of change always involves people, and you can't accomplish your business goals without motivating people. In the past, it was not uncommon to find leaders pushing their teams through negative incentives. "Do this or don't get the promotion." "Do this or you'll get fired." The workforce of tomorrow, and I would argue today, will not tolerate that kind of leadership. Your teams will look for inspiration from you. Employees will expect flexibility and freedom in assignments and working conditions. The greatest leaders will recognize what their teams need and understand that keeping talented employees will mean leading with your heart.

Attracting and retaining top talent is a war. We've seen some of this coming for years. As baby boomers retire, we expect a mass exodus out of the workforce. As millennials have entered the workforce, they are demanding a new kind of leader, one who will value them and provide stimulating work. I point out these two groups, but there are changing dynamics and expectations across the workforce.

One truth of human existence is that we all impact each other, good or bad. Unless you live completely off the grid and never encounter another person, you will be impacted by other human beings surrounding you. I would argue that even in that off the grid place the world is so touched by humans that you cannot avoid it. What I really love about this concept is that we can choose to take the best of people or the worst of them. We choose who we spend time with. We choose how we react to others.

Consider our workforce as an ecosystem that thrives and suffers based on its health as a whole. So, when elements of the workforce are shifting their expectations, demanding new ways of working or finding new meaning in work, we should embrace this as a healthy growth of the ecosystem.

All of this means that as leaders, we need to continue to adapt to the ever-changing workforce. We bring our best to every day and are open to always learning. You are ready to build your leadership skills when you know yourself, are willing to bring your full self to your leadership and are open to continual learning.

As you continually improve your skills, you will undoubtedly read a lot of advice on leadership. There is so much advice for new leaders that you can easily get lost amongst it. One might argue that it couldn't hurt to have more advice than less, but I beg to differ. The reality is that there is so much information that it's easily confusing and contradicting. And every situation is infinitely complex, you can't possibly predict all the scenarios that could go wrong or right.

I've compiled all the advice and my experience into key competencies for every leader to develop that I've detailed in the next few chapters. These are the roadmap to building a solid organization. How you develop these skills and implement them into your work will be particular to your style and situation. But these final chapters can lay the foundation for you to build success as a leader.

15

UNDERSTAND THE STRATEGY CONTINUUM

As a leader, you are responsible for some level of strategy within your organization. At the very top of any organization, we set the vision, mission, and key strategies of the organization. These are often developed with a board of directors or a key leadership team. Occasionally you may find a solo leader setting the vision, mission, and strategy, but it's rarely alone.

As you work your way down through the organization, the overall strategy should cascade into other teams, like a waterfall. No matter where you are in the organization, you should be very clear about where you are in the waterfall and how you are going to lead from that altitude. You have a responsibility to cascade the organization's strategy and feed information back into the leadership ranks to help shape future strategy. The overall strategy should be big picture and probably bold, if you want to get people motivated around it. As you get into the working teams, your strategies should become more detailed, but always aligned with the overall strategy. If your team is rowing against the overall strategy of the organization, you are not leading them in the right direction. Figure out what you need to do to adjust your team's direction to align with the organization.

All too often leaders see their most pressing daily issues and the pressures directly around them. These influences are usually far from the organizational strategies. It's easy to get wrapped up in the day to day pressures. If you do this too long, you'll never get to the strategies your organization has directed. Then you'll only be responding, not leading. This entire situation is one of the biggest mistakes leaders make, and while it might not cause you bad performance reviews it certainly won't get you strategic results. Your team may enjoy working with you and your day to day operations may run smoothly, but you will not be moving your organization forward. There are some roles where this is all that's asked of you. But you need to understand if that's the role you're in. If you are expected to move the organization forward and you're only doing the day to day, you may disappoint your senior leaders.

When it comes to strategy you should follow these simple rules:

1. Be well versed on your organization's strategy
2. Understand your role and how you should be cascading that strategy through your teams

3. Set your team's goals in alignment to the organization's strategy

4. Don't let daily pressures distract you from your strategic goals. Don't get to the end of a year and have made no progress toward your organization's strategy.

Let me tell you a story about David. David led a large non-profit organization. It was easy to get behind the mission of the organization that served underprivileged youth in the community. But the organization did very little strategy planning. They relied on philanthropy to continue to operate their programs with little change from year to year. As a result, they got complacent. They got caught up in the day to day operations. It was easy for a year to go by without thinking strategically. One year, a major fundraiser indicated a significant change in their fundraising process that would cut the funding to David's organization by more than 60%. This step necessitated a formalized planning process to figure out how to respond to the declined funding. It was obvious that the team did not know how to think and plan strategically. The board of directors stepped in to help, but it was late in the year when funding was already cut. Over the course of the next three months, the organization finally went through a thorough strategy assessment and planning process. During the process they uncovered a top-heavy executive budget that was massively inflated compared to other non-profits in the community, and they also found that there were two significant competitors that had entered the market. Over the next five years, David's organization nearly closed after more than

75 years in the community and David and many others were out of work.

Many companies will hire specialists to facilitate their strategic planning processes. This can be a great way to ensure a credible planning model is used and a thorough plan is put in place. But make no mistake…following through with the plan is squarely the responsibility of the business leaders. The planning process should engage the relevant key leaders who will take the charge to cascade the strategy down through the organization. During the process, your facilitator should ensure that the key leaders engage in healthy discussion and hopefully some level of consensus on the strategy. It is much preferred to have this level of engagement with your key levels over just handing down the strategy.

CASCADING YOUR STRATEGY

Each level of your organization will set an annual plan in accordance with the overall strategic plan of the organization. You've probably been involved with these throughout the years. But how often do you create the plan and leave it on the shelf? Be honest.

Organizations that effectively conduct their organizations strategic planning, do better than most at keeping it visible. Almost all will struggle to cascade the strategy. That's because each level of leadership needs education and support to cascade the strategy. All too often you won't get that support. You'll be expected to figure it out.

Good thing you're reading this book!

First, do your best to understand your organization's overall strategy. Study it, ask questions, and listen to how your executives communicate the plans. No matter the level of the organization, if you are leading a team you will be responsible for establishing a plan for your team. What do you hope to accomplish in the coming year? How will you develop your teams?

I like to do this planning as part of a team retreat at least annually. Engage your teams in the process. Help them understand the organization's overall strategy. Guide them to discover with you what actions your team needs to take to work toward the organization's goals. What goals do you have that are specific to your team? Develop a plan that will weave these together into a plan for your team.

I've seen this done very well over the years. My favorite example is within a project management office. The organization had established three major strategies. Each strategy had three main components that were fairly high level, aligned by lines of business. The PMO team aligned their plan by those categories. All the work they did was aligned to one of the organization's strategies or a general category of "business continuity." The latter category was intended for those items that need to get done. We like to call them hygiene projects. If you don't brush your teeth for a day or two, you'll have terrible breath but probably no long-lasting problems. If you don't brush your teeth all year, you'll have major problems. Some of your work is like that. You can't push it off forever.

Software and equipment upgrades are examples of this kind of work.

When your teams come together for your annual planning, take the opportunity to get as much input from your teams as you can. You will undoubtedly get rich information, but you will not necessarily get agreement on your approach. Remember that you are responsible for establishing the roadmap. Be prepared to set that plan.

Once you've set your team's roadmap don't just put it on the shelf. We all know this, but it is very difficult to keep your focus on the roadmap with the daily demands of your work.

But do not fret, you can make it easier. Find ways to weave your roadmap into your daily operations. Keep it front and center. I've seen this done very well when an organization did weekly updates with a dashboard that tied their work to their roadmap. Those weekly updates were work updates regarding daily demands as well as roadmap progress reports. It does not mean that you'll have progress every week. In fact, you likely will not progress your roadmap items quickly. Your roadmap should be key strategies and as such are not going to be easy.

Another great idea is to keep a very visible board of your roadmap. I've seen this done with a bulletin board as you enter your workspace. In today's virtual world you can get creative. How about having your team's goals as your lock screen on your computer or when you login each day? Find a way to incorporate your roadmap into regular communication.

In this way, you and your team will keep working towards your big goals.

When you are leading a team, it is your responsibility to keep focus on the goals. But let's be honest, it's not easy. Those daily demands are sometimes burning piles of crisis! It's all too easy to get pulled into the day to day problems and get swept away in them. You can find yourself six months into the year before you pull your head up to realize you've not made progress. Worse yet, you realize you forgot what your goals were. At a minimum, give yourself a monthly reminder to revisit the goals to keep yourself on course. Make sure they are still relevant, and you set a plan for progress. We are all just human beings after all. You will lose sight of your goals once in a while. Just get back at it as soon as you can.

16

TEAM DEVELOPMENT & SUCCESSION PLANNING

W hen you set your team's goals you will undoubtedly discover that you have some gaps in your current team. You may need more resources to focus on a specific area. You may be overstaffed in another area. Or you may find your current team doesn't have the right skills you need for your plan. Every good plan includes an associated development and succession plan with it.

In many cases, if you are revisiting your goals regularly, you should be able to identify resource risks early. Always be on the lookout for these:

1. Skill gaps: talent you need but don't have.
2. Skill concentrations: talent you have in only one or two people. The "what would you do if they won the lottery and left for Fiji tomorrow?" problem.
3. Overstaffing; Do you have too many people? This

doesn't happen often but can be found and forecasted when changes to your customers' demands or operational efficiencies can decrease the staffing needs.

4. Succession needs. I'll dive into this in the next section.

The development plan is how you are going to develop the skills of your team. Once you've completed a succession assessment of your team, you may find you need to make changes. You should have a development plan with each member of your team. They should own the development plan, but you should hold them accountable to complete it. This doesn't need to be anything fancy. Most organizations do this as part of the annual performance management process. That's fine, but I like to include this as a quarterly review with each team member. You can keep this informal. My style is to have a quarterly coffee conversation with each team member and talk about how they are doing, if their goals have changed, progress they've made, etc. I know other leaders who make this a more formal one on one with documentation each month. I think that's a little often, but I encourage you to find what works for you and your team.

Sometimes your succession planning will uncover more significant changes. This is what I call "Right Setting." More on this later.

SUCCESSION PLANNING

We used to think of succession planning as the work HR does to ensure there is a viable bench of people to take the CEO (or other C-suite roles) when he/she retires or takes a different job.

While you should be doing this kind of work, succession planning is so much more than grooming your next leader. Every team leader should have a succession plan for your team.

First, complete an assessment of each member of your team. I often did this with my leadership team as appropriate. Consider each team member for:

1. Proven performance
2. Potential growth into leadership or advancing technical roles
3. Personal interests
4. Development gaps/options

Group team members into four succession categories:

1. Needs Improvement (may be a new employee or low performer)
2. Steady contributor (solid performance, but lacking advancement capacity)
3. High potential (ready for advancement soon)
4. Ready now

You should have a balance of team members across the spectrum. I find it helpful to use a matrixed heat map to demonstrate visually where your team is at. If you have a lot of your team *Ready Now*, but don't have opportunities available for them you'll need to work on finding motivation and meaningful work for those team members. They are more likely to leave your team for other opportunities as they want to advance their careers.

If you have no one *Ready Now*, you are at risk if you or other leaders leave. Some leaders may think this is not a big problem. You're not planning to leave so why worry about succession planning? Here's the deal, you can love being the big fish and the expert, but if you are always the one your team always comes to aren't you exhausted? In fact, you should be leveraging your team AND building them to potentially lead so you can focus on the truly strategic work that you should be. Remember back to the problem of always getting pulled into daily demands? If you are in an executive role, you should have a competent team around you that takes most of those daily demands. Your job is to remain strategic, keep you focused on the big goals, and secure the future for your organization. You can't do that if you are always dealing with the daily demands.

If this is your life, ask yourself why. Do you have the appropriate structure in place to support the daily demands so you can focus on strategy? Maybe you need to consider hiring an operations director, etc. Do you have people in place, but they still come to you all the time? Ask yourself why this is happening too. A couple of likely scenarios:

1. Make sure your leaders understand the level of autonomy they are expected to use. If they don't have much, change that. EMPOWER your people to deal with those daily demands. Depending on your business this can mean your leaders will have authority over large decisions involving significant dollars. Hire and develop your leaders to handle this responsibility. If you don't trust your leaders to do their job, that's a whole different problem. And it's all yours. You need to develop those leaders or cut them loose. Tough decisions need to be made if you are going to meet your organization's strategic goals.

2. Consider how you get your own energy. Is it possible that you are staying in the daily demands because that's where you are comfortable? I assure you this is very common. No one talks about this because they don't want to admit they are not comfortable in their executive leadership role. They may think they worked so hard to get to this level and it's not what they thought it would be like. Or they may be thinking they really want to be the executive, but they are so accustomed to creating more immediate value answering the day to day demands. It's difficult to see how the strategic leader adds value when you are looking at the daily calendar. You need to be looking at the overall goals, the monthly, quarterly, annual progress that is made doesn't show up on the daily operations reports.

3. If anything in #2 resonates, you may be dealing with a

subproblem. Many leaders struggle in their first year to figure out how to get out of the daily operations and think strategically. When you do figure it out, you may find that your teams keep pulling you back in. Understand that they have been learning to work with you too. If you've been in the daily operations and are trying to pull yourself out, be honest with them about it. They have likely come to expect you to be there. They may be worried about making a decision because you have not empowered them in the past. They've learned bad behavior in that first year. They've been trained to always check with the boss first. If they are always checking with you, you'll keep getting pulled in.

EMPOWER them to make the decisions and try not to second guess them. Support their decisions as much as you can. Over time they will get better and you'll be able to play more strategically. Win-win!

RIGHT SETTING

Let's say you lead a team of programmers. They are skilled in an old technology that you still use but will become obsolete over the next five years. You need team members skills in the latest technology, but you also need to maintain your current systems until they can be retired. What do you do? You need a plan.

You may choose to select a few team members to learn the new technology. These programmers will then build the new tools you'll need. Over time teach the new technology to all your programmers as you switch over your tools and retire the old software. This keeps your existing team, but assumes they are able to learn the new tools and it takes a long time. Unfortunately, we don't usually have a lot of time.

You could choose to hire a small new team to build the new tools and accelerate your teams training and cutover to new systems. This is faster, but expensive. You're also likely to lose more staff as the change is more than some can tolerate. That's not necessarily a bad thing but understand what you're getting into.

One team I worked with was finding the need to adjust a team of project managers into more skilled business strategists. The seasoned project managers on their team had earned the respect of the business as key partners and strategists for new business opportunities due in large part to the specific skill set of the individuals that were hired into those roles. The director had understood that the skills needed were shifting before the jobs actually did, so she hired for the skill.

After the skill need was more evident and accepted by senior leaders the director made the appeal to create new job descriptions and associated recruiting plans to fill the right skills needed for the business. In this scenario, you are changing jobs and holding existing team members to that new job. If the job is significantly different than what they do today you may opt for a swift organization change that will involve team members going through a selection process. This means everyone on the existing team is considered for the new jobs. Some may not meet the new requirements or even want to do that work. In this case, you should work with your HR departments to offer reasonable options including severance for those who choose to leave. This action is drastic for the team but may be the best option long-term for the overall health of your organization. I've experienced this process, even led it, several times. In the end the swift option, if done well, is always best for the remaining team.

In some cases, you may find a need for new roles in addition to your existing teams. In the example above regarding the project managers switching to business strategists, this was the case. We needed to add 3-5 business strategist roles at the same time we needed to maintain our project manager resources. In this case I can fill the business strategist roles by offering the option to those already on the team. Those on the team who are qualified should be considered first, and then hire additional skilled resources. All the while securing everyone's job.

17

ORGANIZATIONAL DESIGN

A s you can probably see, a good organizational design includes strong alignment with the goals of your company and your team. When you are clear where you're going, you have the right jobs and the right people, and you are well on your way. The next thing to consider is the organizational structure.

The most difficult challenge for leaders redesigning their org structure is to do it objectively. You may seek outside counsel to help. When I guide leaders through this process, we always start by taking away all the names. List jobs or roles, not names. I like to use the "furniture placement" method. Use sticky notes for each role you need. Use a single sticky note for each FTE you need. Place the resources into groups along with reporting structures you are considering. For each structure you propose ask yourself the following questions:

1. Does this structure allow the teams to effectively leverage complimentary skills?
2. Does this structure encourage empowered decisions at the appropriate level?
3. Does this structure create barriers to effective decision making or productivity?

Look for problems in the structure at this point rather than discover them after you've made the changes. Put yourself in the shoes of each team member. Are you able to effectively do your job with this structure? Do you have what you need? Do you have the autonomy you need?

Then ask these questions from the perspective of each person on your team. In this way, you can consider different options before you settle on one you'll implement.

Another note on organizational structure...while you don't want to keep changing the structure all the time, most leaders avoid this change longer than they should. I would encourage you to keep an org structure for at least a year, but even with this advice you know your team better than anyone. Do what makes sense for you. The bigger problem I see is leaders not changing the structure when they should. Sometimes, the structure has been in place for so long they can't see anything else. This is actually the time when you really should be shaking it up.

I strongly encourage you to get outside help to brainstorm options in this case. It's so rooted in your team's history that you might not be able to see other options. You may notice team challenges but not associate it with the structure. An outside, objective consultant can help you with this. Organizational design can be one of the most influential factors in the effective communication in a team and ultimately success.

18

CELEBRATING SUCCESS

How often do you celebrate? Do you enjoy a family birthday party? Do you celebrate the big things and the little things? The day my son found the courage to go to a game night with a friend was a big day in our house. I certainly celebrated the hope that he would overcome his crippling shyness! The 30th day I was sober was worth a cake and candles, too! The day my friend found the confidence to apply for the job, we celebrated with a little dance across the living room.

Why should work be any different? In fact, celebrating your successes at work should be commonplace. One of the main reasons people state for discontentment at work is feeling like they are not valued. Celebrating successes and recognizing those who have contributed is important. You let people know that you see them. You acknowledge their contributions. You value them. When your team feels valued, they are more productive, committed, and helpful to their peers. So, when was the last time you celebrated success at work?

I've actually had executives tell me they don't celebrate "too" much. They don't want it to become normal. HA! Why not?!

You can't possibly celebrate too much at work. Remember those daily demands? They won't let you forget. So, celebrate every chance you get. Be creative with it. This is not about celebrating with cake every week at someone's birthday (though I'm all for that, too). This is about taking the time every week to find the things to celebrate; look for the reasons that are right in front of you. Often, the celebrations might seem small to you. I assure you they are not small to your team. You've taken the time to notice. They will notice that.

Ok, so what if you're not the creative type? No worries. There are some great books full of ideas to motivate your teams. Any one of them can spark your creative juices! Or just go ahead and google it. You can certainly find some innovative and interesting ideas if you just take the time to look. I also like to ask my team or colleagues for ideas. Just tell them what you want to celebrate and ask for their great ideas. They'll surprise you!

Trust me, I've been surprised by so much in my life that I now expect that the people around me will give me some new knowledge all the time. For this reason, I can find comfort in the uncertainty, but more importantly joy in the journey. It's no different for me at work. I want to work with wonderful people, so I seek out those clients and partners. When I worked in the corporate world, I surrounded myself with teams of diverse perspectives and experiences that would continually push me and yes, surprise me. I encourage you to do the same. And when it's time to celebrate, get everyone involved.

19

CREATING A CULTURE

All this talk about celebrating has me thinking about creating a culture in your teams. Yes, you get to create the culture, isn't it great! Every organization will have a culture of its own. If it's your company, you definitely lead the culture, but even if you are a leader among many you still have the power to lead your culture.

When I worked for a large healthcare provider, the culture of the organization was a strong culture of values focused on service, integrity, and care for our patients above all else. But as with any large organization, you will find micro-cultures in every team. When an organization has done a great job of instilling their values into their teams, you'll find those values along with others the team brings. The team leaders and other team members will feed the culture with their own beliefs. So, what do you feed your team's culture? Your approach to leadership will drastically affect the team culture. You can probably think of a leader you've had in the past who created a culture of fear or complacency or <fill in your experience>. It's important for you to be aware of the kind of culture you create. If you don't know, get some feedback. All of us create a culture in our teams. Do your best to make it a good one!

What if you find yourself in a culture that you want to change? It might not necessarily signal a negative culture. I once consulted with a company who needed to lead their teams through a significant transformation that required everyone in the business to think differently. This is huge and requires a culture change. So, what do you do? In this case, you may want to consider a change management consultant that can help you work through all the changes needed. Culture is not changed by one action or one speech/declaration. Culture changes over time and with a lot of work. It will take a series of communication, action, and incentives across the teams. You might need some help with all that from an expert.

But what if you are a new leader and you want to create a more inclusive culture? Or correct a negative culture? Here is the greatest news...you lead the culture as the leader. The team will look to you. Set the example you want of the team.

Correct discretions quickly in others and in yourself. Set your expectations for the kind of culture you want to create and talk about them often. Take feedback and input from your teams as they adjust to the new culture. This will take time. One leader once told me it takes at least 18 months to change a culture. I think you must find ways to change more quickly in today's world, but the point he intended still stands...it takes time for people to adjust to change. Don't expect it to change overnight. Help your teams adjust to your expectations by listening to their concerns along the way. Answer their concerns as much and often as you can. This will help you change the culture and lead the team to the success you intend.

20

SO NOW WHAT?

I spent 25 years climbing a corporate ladder while trying to be a mom and a wife. You know from my story that my journey may have not been picture perfect, but it has been perfectly what I needed it to be. I've shared much of my leadership knowledge, lessons, and practical advice with you here, but I want my most important message to not be missed. So, let's make it very clear...

Be Yourself!!!

Learn everything you can, make mistakes, and celebrate your successes; but don't ever try to be someone you are not. Know that at the end of our days we will look back on our lives. No matter what, be proud to have done it your own way. Love yourself. Be yourself. Inspire others to be themselves.

I consider myself a very confident person now. In fact, I've been told that I can be intimidating. I live out loud. I'm bold (most of the time). In many parts of my life, this is my gift that I want to share with others. I know my confidence can be infectious. But it's not for everyone. In fact, my dear husband is very different from me. Thank god! He has a quiet confidence. He is my rock. But it's not always easy. We love each other deeply, but we couldn't be more different. And it works. In every relationship you need to have something in common, but it's in the differences where the passion and excitement is. I can find myself quickly overtaking the space with my husband. I need to take responsibility for my actions that don't create that space for him. When I'm aware of myself I'm a better wife, friend, leader, and person. I wish that for you too.

I truly believe that every great leader needs to start by being a good person. Not a perfect person, just a good person. No one is perfect, and no life is perfect. In fact, most of us are pretty messed up when you get down to it. We carry a lot of baggage along with us. Throughout this book I've spilled my life story with all the ugly details, and you kept reading (thank you).

But I need to tell you that I carried that baggage far too long. Don't make the same mistake. Unpack that shit. Leave it on the curb, and move on.

I want you to learn from all my mistakes. I want you to also be inspired to be better. I hope you are inspired to help others or inspired in the wisdom that you have something to offer that is uniquely yours. Give it freely to this world and to your teams. My mission is to inspire scores of women to step into their power and lead our world to better things. You will lead our communities and organizations into the future. You will create better families and raise children to be better people. The world is waiting for your next big move!

Once you've taken to heart the need for self-awareness, you've absorbed the lessons from others, and you've accepted you'll always be learning, you're ready to take on the world! Go forth and conquer, my friend! This world needs you. And when you need a little help, call on your coaches, advisors, and mentors to help you along the way.

Whatever compelled you to pick up this book is within you; maybe it was a desire to learn, to be better, to solve problems, or to feel satisfaction. I truly hope you've found something in these pages that will cause you to examine how you lead, how you team, how you parent, how you love, and how you give your gift to the world.

Embrace your story, be your whole self unapologetically, lead boldly, and change the world.

You've Got This!

ACKNOWLEDGMENTS

Special thanks to my wonderful family.

Your unconditional support means more than you'll ever know.

To Jeff for your steady support even when my dreams seem a little crazy.

To Gabby for reminding me the power of my voice and to be proud of who I am.

To Chris for your vulnerability and gentle soul, always reminding me to be grateful every day for those you love most.

A special thank you to my grammar-correcting friend Jen. You gave me your gifts to make this book happen and your encouragement to survive the process!

ABOUT THE AUTHOR

Nicky Espinosa is a Midwest girl through and through, where she currently lives with her husband and three dogs. As a young girl growing up on a hobby farm in Minnesota Nicky always dreamed big and moved fast. She fell in love with her husband at first sight and has been married for over 25 years. She raised two children while climbing the corporate ladder before launching a successful coaching business. In her corporate life Nicky built a successful career as a healthcare executive leading teams, guiding strategy and advising executives. Nicky's mission is to inspire more women to confidently step into leadership and influence positive change. Nicky is always having fun and embracing the unexpected. She enjoys driving with the windows down and the music loud and lives by the motto: always act younger than you are. In her first book, *No Apology Needed*, Nicky encourages you to embrace your wilder side and step up to your badass influence to create the career of your dreams. The only limits are the ones you create!

CONNECT WITH NICKY ESPINOSA

Book a call with Nicky: www.espinosacoaching.com

Join our Facebook Community for regular messages directly
from Nicky!
https://www.facebook.com/
groups/badassconfidentwomenleaders

Contact Nicky directly: Nicky@espinosacoaching.com

Made in the USA
Monee, IL
20 October 2021